SPOTLIGHT

D0179196

BANFF
NATIONAL PARK

ANDREW HEMPSTEAD

Contents

BANFF
NATIONAL PARK

BANFF NATIONAL PARK

This 6,641-square-kilometer (2,564-square-mile) national park encompasses some of the world's most magnificent scenery. The snow-capped peaks of the Rocky Mountains form a spectacular backdrop for glacial lakes, fast-flowing rivers, and endless forests. Deer, moose, elk, mountain goats, bighorn sheep, black and grizzly bears, wolves, and cougars inhabit the park's vast wilderness, while the human species is concentrated in the picture-postcard towns of Banff and Lake Louise—two of North America's most famous resorts. Banff is near the park's southeast gate, 128 kilometers (80 miles) west of Calgary. Lake Louise, northwest of Banff along the TransCanada Highway, sits astride its namesake lake, which is regarded as one of the seven natural wonders of the world. The lake is rivaled for sheer beauty only by Moraine Lake, just down the road. Just north of Lake Louise, the Icefields Parkway begins its spectacular course alongside the Continental Divide to Jasper National Park.

One of Banff's greatest draws is the accessibility of its natural wonders. Most highlights are close to the road system, but adventurous visitors can follow an excellent system of hiking trails to alpine lakes, along glacial valleys, and to spectacular viewpoints where crowds are scarce and human impact has been minimal. Summer in the park is busy. In fact, the park receives nearly half of its four million annual visitors in just two months (July and August). The rest of the year, crowds outside the town of Banff are negligible. In winter, three world-class winter resorts—Ski Norquay, Sunshine Village, and Lake Louise (Canada's second-largest winter

© ANDREW HEMPSTEAD

HIGHLIGHTS

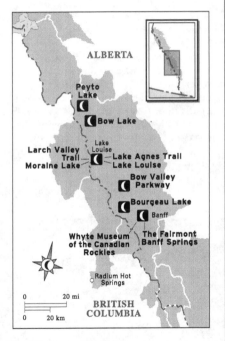

《 Whyte Museum of the Canadian Rockies: If you visit only one museum in Banff, make it this one for a snapshot of the park's human history (page 22).

《 The Fairmont Banff Springs: You don't need to book a room here to enjoy the many wonders of one of the world's great mountain resorts – join a guided tour, enjoy a meal, or simply wander through the grandiose public areas (page 25).

《 Bow Valley Parkway: This scenic drive between Banff and Lake Louise provides views of abundant wildlife and many worthwhile stops (page 29).

《 Bourgeau Lake: A steep trail leads to this lake's rocky shores, populated by colonies of pikas (page 37).

《 Lake Louise: Famous Lake Louise has hypnotized visitors with her beauty for over 100 years. Visitors can rent canoes from the boathouse (page 67).

《 Moraine Lake: If anywhere in the Canadian Rockies qualified as a Double Must-See, it would be this deep-blue body of water surrounded by glaciated peaks (page 70).

《 Lake Agnes Trail: You won't completely escape the crowds by hiking this trail from Lake Louise, but you will leave most of them behind (page 72).

《 Larch Valley Trail: This walk is a good introduction to hiking in the Canadian Rockies, especially in fall when the larch trees have turned a brilliant gold (page 73).

《 Bow Lake: Although you can soak up this lake's beauty from the Icefields Parkway, walk along its northern shoreline early in the morning to make the most of this scenic gem (page 84).

《 Peyto Lake: Another one of Banff's famous lakes. The main difference is the perspective from which it is viewed – a lookout high above its shoreline (page 84).

LOOK FOR **《** TO FIND RECOMMENDED SIGHTS, ACTIVITIES, DINING, AND LODGING.

resort)—crank up their lifts. During this low season, hotel rates are reasonable. If you tire of downhill skiing and snowboarding, you can try cross-country skiing, ice-skating, or snowshoeing; take a sleigh ride; soak in a hot spring; or go heli-skiing nearby.

The park is open year-round, although occasional road closures occur on mountain passes along the park's western boundary in winter, due to avalanche-control work and snowstorms.

PLANNING YOUR TIME

If you are planning to visit the Canadian Rockies, it is almost inevitable that your itinerary will include Banff National Park, both for its many and varied outdoor attractions and for its central location. The park can be anything you want it to be, depending on the time of year you visit and what your interests are. The main population center is Banff, which has all the services of a large town, as well as attractions such as landmark **Fairmont Banff Springs** hotel and the **Whyte Museum of the**

Canadian Rockies. The park holds four lakes that you won't want to miss for their scenic beauty: **Lake Louise, Moraine Lake, Bow,** and **Peyto.** All four are easily accessible by road but also offer surrounding hiking, and the former two have canoe rentals. Hiking is the park's biggest attraction, and many visitors plan their itinerary around it. I'd suggest mixing it up—choosing from the hikes that reflect your fitness level and combining them with visits to the major natural attractions. For example, when in the vicinity of Lake Louise, walk the **Lake Agnes Trail,** and while at Moraine Lake, plan on visiting **Larch Valley.** For the more adventurous, **Bourgeau Lake** is a stunning day-hike destination.

You can book one accommodation for your entire stay or spend an equal number of nights in Banff and Lake Louise. If you have a family or like the convenience of staying put for your entire vacation, it is practical to book a room in either Banff or Lake Louise and use it as a base—spending your days in the park but also venturing farther afield, with, for example, one

Lake Louise

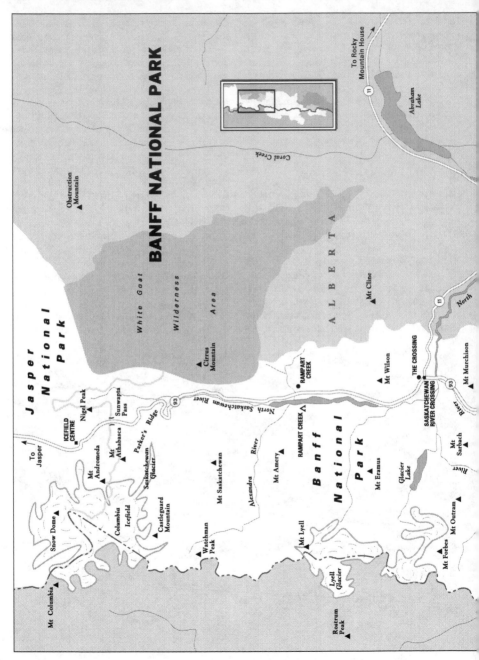

© AVALON TRAVEL

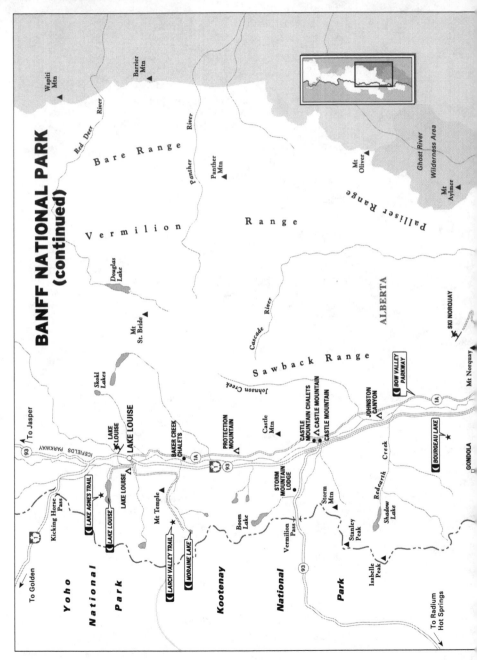

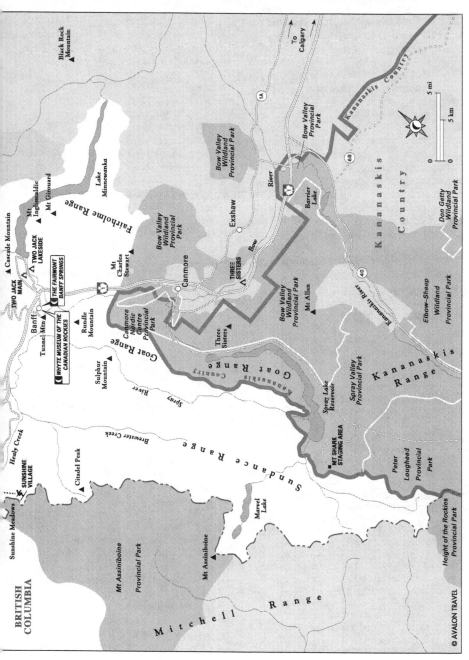

© AVALON TRAVEL

day scheduled for Yoho National Park and another for a Canmore/Kananaskis combo.

Unless you're a die-hard skier or snowboarder, summer is definitely the best time of year to visit. The months of July and August are the busiest, with crowds decreasing exponentially in the weeks before and after these two months. June and September are wonderful times to visit the park. Aside from the crowd factor, in June, wildflowers start blooming and wildlife is abundant. September sees temperatures ripe for hiking, and the turning colors are at their peak. In either month, discounted accommodations are a welcome bonus. In May and October–November, the park is at its quietest. Temperatures in any of these three months are generally too cool for hiking (although welcome warm spells are common). The park's three alpine resorts begin opening in December and remain in operation

PARK ENTRY

Permits are required for entry into Banff National Park. A **National Parks Day Pass** is adult $9.80, senior $8.30, child $4.90 to a maximum of $20 per vehicle. It is interchangeable between parks and is valid until 4 P.M. the day following its purchase.

An annual **National Parks of Canada Pass,** good for entry into national parks across Canada, is adult $53, senior $45, child $27, to a maximum of $107 per vehicle. History buffs may find a **Discovery Package** worth the money. For adult $85, senior $73, child $42, to a maximum of $166 per vehicle, it allows unlimited entry to national parks and national historic sites (two of which are in Banff National Park) for a full year from the date of purchase.

All passes can be bought at the eastern park gate on the TransCanada Highway, the park information centers in Banff or Lake Louise, and at campground kiosks. For more information, check online at the Parks Canada website (www.pc.gc.ca).

until April or May. While skiing and boarding are the big wintertime draw, plan on expanding your experience by joining a sleigh ride, trying snowshoeing, or heading out ice fishing.

THE LAND

The park lies within the main and front ranges of the Rocky Mountains, a mountain range that extends the length of the North American continent. Although the mountains are composed of bedrock laid down up to one billion years ago, it wasn't until 100 million years ago that forces below the earth's surface transformed the lowland plain of what is now western Canada into the varied, mountainous topography we see today.

The front ranges lie to the east, bordering the foothills. These geologically complex mountains are made up of younger bedrock that has been folded, faulted, and uplifted. The main ranges are older and higher, with the bedrock lying mainly horizontal and not as severely disturbed as the front ranges. Here the pressures have been most powerful; these mountains are characterized by castlelike buttresses and pinnacles, and warped waves of stratified rock. Most glaciers are found among these lofty peaks. The spine of the main range is the **Continental Divide.** In Canadian latitudes to the east of the divide, all waters flow to the Atlantic Ocean; those to the west flow into the Pacific.

Since rising above the surrounding plains, these mountains have been eroding. At least four times in the last million years sheets of ice have covered much of the land. Advancing and retreating back and forth like steel wool across the landscape, they rounded off lower peaks and carved formerly V-shaped valleys into broad U-shaped ones (**Bow Valley** is the most distinctive). Meanwhile, glacial meltwater continued carving ever-deeper channels into the valleys, and rivers changed course many times.

This long history of powerful and even violent natural events over the eons has left behind the dramatic landscape visitors marvel over today. Now forming the exposed sides of many a mountain peak, layers of drastically altered sediment are visible from miles away, especially when accentuated by a particular angle of sunlight or a light fall of snow. **Cirques,** gouged into the mountains by glacial action, fill with glacial meltwater each spring, creating trademark translucent green lakes that will take your breath away. The wide, sweeping U-shaped valleys scoured out by glaciers past now create magnificent panoramas that will draw you to pull off the road and gasp in awe; open views are easy to come by here, thanks to a climate that keeps the tree line low.

FLORA

Nearly 700 species of plants have been recorded in the park. Each species falls into one of three distinct vegetation zones, based primarily on altitude. Lowest is the montane zone, which covers the valley floor. Above it, the subalpine zone comprises most of the forested area. Highest of all is the alpine zone, where climate is severe and vegetation cover is limited.

Montane-zone vegetation is usually found at elevations below 1,350 meters (4,430 feet) but can grow at higher elevations on sun-drenched, south-facing slopes. Because fires frequently affect this zone, **lodgepole pine** is the dominant species; its tightly sealed cones only open with the heat of a forest fire, thereby regenerating the species quickly after a blaze. **Douglas fir** is the zone's climax species and is found in open stands, such as on Tunnel Mountain. **Aspen** is common in older burn areas, while **limber pine** thrives on rocky outcrops.

Dense forests of **white spruce** and **Engelmann spruce** typify the subalpine zone. White spruce dominates up to 2,100 meters (6,890 feet); above 2,100 meters (6,890 feet) to 2,400 meters (7,870 feet), Engelmann spruce is dominant. In areas affected by fire, such as west of Castle Junction, lodgepole pine occurs in dense stands. **Subalpine fir** grows above 2,200 meters (7,550 feet) and is often stunted by the high winds experienced at such lofty elevations.

The transition from subalpine to alpine is gradual and usually occurs around 2,300 meters (7,560 feet). The alpine has a severe climate, with temperatures averaging below zero. Low temperatures, strong winds, and a very short summer force alpine plants to adapt by growing low to the ground with long roots. Mosses, mountain avens, saxifrage, and an alpine dandelion all thrive in this environment. The best place to view the brightly colored carpet of **alpine flowers** is at Sunshine Meadows or Parker's Ridge.

FAUNA

Viewing the park's abundant and varied wildlife is one of the most popular visitor activities in Banff. In summer, with the onslaught of the tourist hordes, many of the larger mammals move away from the heavily traveled areas. It then becomes a case of knowing when and where to look for them. Spring and fall are the best times of year for wildlife viewing; the crowds are thinner than in summer, and big-game animals are more likely to be seen at lower elevations. Winter also has its advantages. Although **bears** are hibernating, a large herd of **elk** winters on the outskirts of the town of Banff, **coyotes** are often seen roaming around town, **bighorn sheep** have descended from the heights, and **wolf** packs can be seen along the Bow Valley Corridor.

Small Mammals

One of the first mammals you're likely to come in contact with is the **Columbian ground squirrel,** seen throughout the park's lower elevations. The **golden-mantled ground squirrel,** similar in size but with a striped back, is common at higher elevations or around rocky outcrops. The one collecting Engelmann spruce cones is the **red squirrel.** The **least chipmunk** is striped, but it's smaller than the golden-mantled squirrel. It lives in dry, rocky areas throughout the park.

Short-tailed weasels are common, but **long-tailed weasels** are rare. Look for both in higher subalpine forests. **Pikas** (commonly called rock rabbits) and **hoary marmots** (well known for their shrill whistles) live among rock slides near high-country lakes: look for them around Moraine Lake and along Bow Summit

THE ELK OF BANFF NATIONAL PARK

Few visitors leave Banff without having seen elk – a large member of the deer family easily distinguished by its white rump. Though the animals have been reported passing through the park for a century, they've never been indigenous. In 1917, 57 elk were moved to Banff from Yellowstone National Park. Two years later, 20 more were transplanted, and the new herd multiplied rapidly. At that time, coyotes, cougars, and wolves were being slaughtered under a predator-control program, leaving the elk unfettered by nature's population-control mechanisms. The elk proliferated and soon became a problem as they took to wintering in the range of bighorn sheep, deer, moose, and beaver. Between 1941 and 1969, controlled slaughters of elk were conducted in an attempt to reduce the population.

Today, with wolf packs returning to the park, the elk population has stabilized at about 2,800. In summer, look for them in open meadows along the Bow Valley Parkway, along the road to Two Jack Lake, or at Vermilion Lakes.

Each fall, traditionally, hundreds of elk moved into the town itself, but starting in recent years, Parks Canada has been making a concerted effort to keep them away from areas such as the golf course and recreation grounds. The main reason for this is that fall is rutting season, and the libidinal bull elk become dangerous as they gather their harems.

You may still see the odd elk feeding in downtown Central Park or walking proudly down Banff Avenue, but it's more likely you'll spot one on the outskirts of town.

© ANDREW HEMPSTEAD

Loop. **Porcupines** are widespread and are most active at night.

Vermilion Lakes is an excellent place to view the **beaver** at work; the best time is dawn or dusk. **Muskrats** and **mink** are common in all wetlands within the park.

Hoofed Residents

The most common and widespread of the park's hoofed residents are **elk,** which number around 2,800. Starting in 2000, a concerted effort was made to keep them out of Banff's downtown core, but they are still congregating around the outskirts of the town, including up near the Tunnel Mountain campgrounds. They can also be seen along the Bow Valley Parkway. **Moose** were once common around Vermilion Lakes, but competition from an artificially expanded elk population caused their numbers to decline, and now only around 100 live in the park. Look for them at Waterfowl Lakes and along the Icefields Parkway near Rampart Creek.

Mule deer, named for their large ears, are most common in the southern part of the park. Watch for them along the Mount Norquay Road and Bow Valley Parkway. **White-tailed deer** are much less common but are seen occasionally at Saskatchewan River Crossing. A small herd of around 20 **woodland caribou** remains in the Dolomite Pass area and Upper Pipestone Valley and is rarely seen.

It is estimated that the park is home to around 900 **mountain goats.** These nimble-footed creatures occupy all mountain peaks, living almost the entire year in the higher subalpine and alpine regions. The most accessible place to view these high-altitude hermits is along Parker's Ridge in the far northwestern corner of the park. The park's **bighorn sheep** have for the most part lost their fear of humans and often congregate at certain spots to lick salt from the road. Your best chance of seeing one of the park's 2,000–2,300 bighorn is at the south end of the Bow Valley Parkway, between switchbacks on Mount Norquay Road, and between Lake Minnewanka and Two Jack Lake.

Wild Dogs and Cats

Coyotes are widespread along the entire Bow River watershed. They are attracted to Vermilion Lakes by an abundance of small game, and many have permanent dens there. **Wolves** had been driven close to extinction by the early 1950s, but today at least four wolf packs have been reported in the park. One pack winters close to town and is occasionally seen on Vermilion Lakes during that period. The **lynx** population fluctuates greatly; look for them in the backcountry during winter. **Cougars** are shy and number fewer than 20 in the park. They are occasionally seen along the front ranges behind Cascade Mountain.

Bears

The exhilaration of seeing one of these magnificent creatures in its natural habitat is unforgettable. From the road you're most likely to see **black bears,** which actually range in color from jet black to cinnamon brown and number around 50. Try the Bow Valley Parkway at dawn or late in the afternoon. Farther north they are occasionally seen near the road as it passes Cirrus Mountain. Banff's 60-odd **grizzly bears** spend most of the year in remote valleys, often on south-facing slopes away from the Bow Valley Corridor. During late spring they are occasionally seen in residential areas, along the Lake Minnewanka loop road, on the golf course, and in the area of Bow Pass.

The chance of encountering a bear face-to-face in the backcountry is remote. To lessen chances even further, you should take some simple precautions: Never hike alone or at dusk. Make lots of noise when passing through heavy vegetation. Keep a clean camp. Read the pamphlets available at all park visitors centers. At the Banff Visitor Centre (224 Banff Ave.), daily trail reports list all recent bear sightings. Report any bears you see to the Warden's Office (403/762-4506).

Reptiles and Amphibians

The **wandering garter snake** is rare and found only near the Cave and Basin, where warm water from the mineral spring flows down a shaded slope into Vermilion Lakes. Amphibians found in the park include the widespread **western toad;** the **wood frog,** commonly found along the Bow River; the rare **spotted frog;** and the **long-toed salamander,** which spawns in shallow ponds and spends summer under logs or rocks in the vicinity of its spawning grounds.

Birds

Although more than 240 species of birds have been recorded in the park, most are shy and live in heavily wooded areas. One species that definitely isn't shy is the fearless **gray jay,** which haunts all campgrounds and picnic areas. Similar in color, but larger, is the **Clark's nutcracker,** which lives in higher, subalpine forests. Another common bird is the black and white **magpie. Ravens** are frequently encountered, especially around campgrounds.

Several species of **woodpecker** live in subalpine forests. A number of species of grouse are also in residence. Most common is the **downy ruffed grouse** seen in montane forest. The **blue grouse** and **spruce grouse** are seen at higher elevations, as is the **white-tailed ptarmigan,** which lives above the tree line. (Watch for them in Sunshine Meadows or on the Bow Summit Loop.) A colony of **black swifts** in Johnston Canyon is one of only two in the Canadian Rockies.

Good spots to view **dippers** and migrating waterfowl are Hector Lake, Vermilion Lakes, and the wetland area near Muleshoe Picnic Area. A bird blind has been set up below the Cave and Basin but is only worth visiting at dawn and dusk when the hordes of human visitors aren't around. Part of the nearby marsh stays ice free during winter, attracting **killdeer** and other birds.

Although raptors are not common in the park, **bald eagles** and **golden eagles** are present part of the year, and Alberta's provincial bird, the **great horned owl,** lives in the park year-round.

HISTORY

Although the valleys of the Canadian Rockies became ice free nearly 8,000 years ago and native people periodically have hunted in the area since that time, the story of Banff National Park really began with the arrival of the railroad to the area.

The Coming of the Railway

In 1871, Canadian prime minister John A. MacDonald promised to build a rail line linking British Columbia to the rest of the country as a condition of the new province joining the confederation. It wasn't until early 1883 that the line reached Calgary, pushing through to **Laggan,** now known as Lake Louise, that fall. The rail line was one of the largest and costliest engineering jobs ever undertaken in Canada.

Discovery of the Cave and Basin

On November 8, 1883, three young railway workers—Franklin McCabe and William and Thomas McCardell—went prospecting for gold on their day off. After crossing the Bow River by raft, they came across a warm stream and traced it to its source at a small log-choked basin of warm water that had a distinct smell of sulphur. Nearby they detected the source of the foul smell coming from a hole in the ground. Nervously, one of the three men lowered himself into the hole and came across a subterranean pool of aqua green warm water. The three men had found not gold, but something just as precious—a hot mineral spring that in time would attract wealthy customers from around the world. Word of the discovery soon got out, and the government encouraged visitors to the Cave and Basin as an ongoing source of revenue to support the new railway.

A 2,500-hectare (6,177-acre) reserve was established around the springs on November 25, 1885, and two years later the reserve was expanded and renamed **Rocky Mountains Park.** It was primarily a business enterprise centered around the unique springs and catering to wealthy patrons of the railway. At the turn of the 20th century, Canada had an abundance of wilderness; it certainly didn't need a park to preserve it. The only goal of Rocky Mountains Park was to generate income for the government and the Canadian Pacific Railway (CPR).

WILD BILL PEYTO

These words from a friend sum up Bill Peyto – one of Banff's earliest characters and one of the Canadian Rockies' greatest guides: "rarely speaking – his forte was doing things, not talking about them." In 1886, at the tender age of 18, Ebenezer William Peyto left England for Canada. After traveling extensively he settled in Banff and was hired as an apprentice guide for legendary outfitter Tom Wilson. Wearing a tilted sombrero, fringed buckskin coat, cartridge belt, hunting knife, and six-shooter, he looked more like a gunslinger than a mountain man.

As his reputation as a competent guide grew, so did the stories. While guiding clients on one occasion, he led them to his cabin. Before entering, Peyto threw stones in the front door until a loud snap was heard. It was a bear trap that he'd set up to catch a certain trapper who'd been stealing his food. One of the guests commented that if caught, the trapper would surely have died. "You're damned right he would have," Bill replied. "Then I'd have known for sure it was him."

In 1900, Peyto left Banff to fight in the Boer War and was promoted to corporal for bravery. This title was revoked before it became official after the army officials learned he'd "borrowed" an officer's jacket and several bottles of booze for the celebration. Returning to a hero's welcome in Banff, Peyto established an outfitting business and continued prospecting for copper in Simpson Pass. Although his outfitting business thrived, the death of his wife left him despondent. He built a house on Banff Avenue; its name, "Ain't it Hell," summed up his view of life.

In his later years, he became a warden in the Healy Creek-Sunshine district, where his exploits during the 1920s added to his already legendary name. After 20 years of service he retired, and in 1943, at the age of 75, he passed away. One of the park's most beautiful lakes is named after him, as are a glacier and a popular Banff watering hole (Wild Bill's – a designation he would have appreciated). His face also adorns the large signs welcoming visitors to Banff.

A Town Grows

After the discovery of the Cave and Basin across the Bow River from the railway station (then known as Siding 29), many commercial facilities sprang up along what is now Banff Avenue. The general manager of the CPR (later to become its vice president), William Cornelius Van Horne, was instrumental in creating a hotel business along the rail line. His most recognized achievement was the Banff Springs Hotel, which opened in 1888. It was the world's largest hotel at the time. Enterprising locals soon realized the area's potential and began opening restaurants, offering guided hunting and boating trips, and developing manicured gardens. Banff soon became Canada's best-known tourist resort, attracting visitors from around the world. It was named after Banffshire, the Scottish birthplace of George Stephen, the CPR's first president.

In 1902, the park boundary was again expanded to include 11,440 square kilometers (4,417 square miles) of the Canadian Rockies. This dramatic expansion meant that the park became not just a tourist resort but also home to existing coal-mining and logging operations and hydroelectric dams. Government officials saw no conflict of interest, actually stating that the coal mine and township at Bankhead added to the park's many attractions. Many of the forests were logged, providing wood for construction, while other areas were burned to allow clear sightings for surveyors' instruments.

After a restriction on automobiles in the park was lifted in 1916, Canada's best-known tourist resort also became its busiest. More and more commercial facilities sprang up, offering luxury and opulence amid the wilderness of the Canadian Rockies. Calgarians built summer cottages, and the town began advertising itself as a year-round destination. As attitudes began to change, the government set up a Dominion Parks Branch, whose first commissioner, J. B. Hawkins, believed that land set aside for parks should be used for recreation and education. Gradually, resource industries were phased out. Hawkins's work culminated in the National Parks Act of 1930, which in turn led Rocky Mountains Park to be renamed Banff National Park. The park's present boundaries, encompassing 6,641 square kilometers (2,564 square miles), were established in 1964.

Icefields Parkway

Natives and early explorers found the swampy nature of the Bow Valley north of Lake Louise difficult for foot and horse travel. When heading north, they used instead the Pipestone River Valley to the east. Banff guide Bill Peyto led American explorer Walter Wilcox up the Bow Valley in 1896, to the high peaks along the Continental Divide northeast of Lake Louise. The first complete journey along this route was made by Jim Brewster in 1904. Soon after, A. P. Coleman made the arduous journey, becoming a strong supporter for the route aptly

known as The Wonder Trail. During the Great Depression of the 1930s, as part of a relief-work project, construction began on what was to become the Icefields Parkway. The road was completed in 1939, and the first car traveled the route in 1940. In tribute to the excellence of the road's early construction, the original roadbed, when upgraded to its present standard in 1961, was followed nearly the entire way.

Town of Banff

For most of its existence, the town of Banff was run as a service center for park visitors by the Canadian Parks Service in Ottawa, a government department with plenty of economic resources but little idea about how to handle the day-to-day running of a midsized town. Any inconvenience this arrangement caused park residents was offset by cheap rent and subsidized services. In June 1988, Banff's residents voted to sever this tie, and on January 1, 1990, Banff officially became an incorporated town, no different than any other in Alberta (except that Parks Canada controls environmental protection within the town of Banff).

Town of Banff

Many visitors planning a trip to the national park don't realize that the town of Banff is a bustling commercial center. The town's location is magnificent. It is spread out along the Bow River, extending to the lower slopes of Sulphur Mountain to the south and Tunnel Mountain to the east. In one direction is the towering face of Mount Rundle, and in the other, framed by the buildings along Banff Avenue, is Cascade Mountain. Hotels and motels line the north end of Banff Avenue, while a profusion of shops, boutiques, cafés, and restaurants hugs the south end. Also at the south end, just over the Bow River, is the Park Administration Building. Here the road forks—to the right is the historic Cave and Basin Hot Springs, to the left the Fairmont Banff Springs and Banff Gondola. Some

people are happy walking along the crowded streets or shopping in a unique setting; those more interested in some peace and quiet can easily slip into pristine wilderness just a five-minute walk from town.

SIGHTS AND DRIVES
Banff Park Museum

Although displays of stuffed animals are not usually associated with national parks, the Banff Park Museum (93 Banff Ave., 403/762-1558, 10 A.M.–6 P.M. daily mid-May–Sept., 1–5 P.M. daily the rest of the year, adult $4, senior $3.50, child $3) provides an insight into the park's early history. Visitors during the Victorian era were eager to see the park's animals without actually having to venture into the bush. A lack of roads and scarcity of

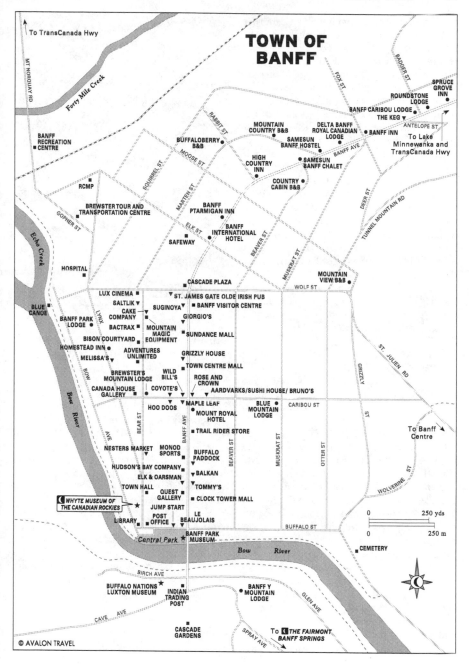

TOWN OF BANFF

To TransCanada Hwy

MT NORQUAY RD
Forty Mile Creek

BANFF RECREATION CENTRE

RCMP

BREWSTER TOUR AND TRANSPORTATION CENTRE

GOPHER ST

Echo Creek

HOSPITAL

BLUE CANOE

Bow River

SQUIRREL ST

MOOSE ST

MARTEN ST

ELK ST

RABBIT ST

BUFFALOBERRY B&B

MOUNTAIN COUNTRY B&B

SAMESUN BANFF HOSTEL

HIGH COUNTRY INN

BANFF PTARMIGAN INN

BANFF INTERNATIONAL HOTEL

SAFEWAY

COUNTRY CABIN B&B

CASCADE PLAZA

BEAVER ST

MUSKRAT ST

DELTA BANFF ROYAL CANADIAN LODGE

SAMESUN BANFF CHALET

DEER ST

TUNNEL MOUNTAIN RD

FOX ST

BADGER ST

SPRUCE GROVE INN

ROUNDSTONE LODGE

BANFF CARIBOU LODGE

THE KEG

BANFF INN

ANTELOPE ST

BANFF AVE

To Lake Minnewanka and TransCanada Hwy

MOUNTAIN VIEW B&B

WOLF ST

LUX CINEMA
SALTLIK
CAKE COMPANY
BACTRAX
BISON COURTYARD
HOMESTEAD INN
MELISSA'S

LYNX

BANFF PARK LODGE

ST. JAMES GATE OLDE IRISH PUB
BANFF VISITOR CENTRE
SUGINOYA
GIORGIO'S
MOUNTAIN MAGIC EQUIPMENT
SUNDANCE MALL
GRIZZLY HOUSE
TOWN CENTRE MALL

ADVENTURES UNLIMITED

BREWSTER'S MOUNTAIN LODGE
CANADA HOUSE GALLERY

BOW AVE

WILD BILL'S
COYOTE'S

HOO DOOS

BEAR ST

ROSE AND CROWN
AARDVARKS/SUSHI HOUSE/ BRUNO'S

MAPLE LEAF
MOUNT ROYAL HOTEL

BLUE MOUNTAIN LODGE

CARIBOU ST

TRAIL RIDER STORE

BANFF AVE

NESTERS MARKET
HUDSON'S BAY COMPANY
ELK & OARSMAN
TOWN HALL

MONOD SPORTS

QUEST GALLERY

JUMP START

WHYTE MUSEUM OF THE CANADIAN ROCKIES

LIBRARY

POST OFFICE

BUFFALO PADDOCK
BALKAN
TOMMY'S
CLOCK TOWER MALL

LE BEAUJOLAIS

BANFF PARK MUSEUM

Central Park

BEAVER ST

MUSKRAT ST

OTTER ST

ST. JULIEN RD

GRIZZLY ST

WOLVERINE ST

To Banff Centre

BUFFALO ST

CEMETERY

0   250 yds
0   250 m

Bow River

BIRCH AVE

BUFFALO NATIONS LUXTON MUSEUM

INDIAN TRADING POST

BANFF Y MOUNTAIN LODGE

GLEN AVE

CAVE AVE

CASCADE GARDENS

SPRAY AVE

To THE FAIRMONT BANFF SPRINGS

© AVALON TRAVEL

large game resulting from hunting meant that the best places to see animals, stuffed or otherwise, were the game paddock, the zoo, and this museum, which was built in 1903. In its early years, the Banff Zoo and Aviary occupied the grounds behind the museum. The zoo kept more than 60 species of animals, including a polar bear. The museum itself was built before the park had electricity, hence the railroad pagoda design using skylights on all levels.

As times changed, the museum was considered outdated; plans for its demolition were put forward in the 1950s. Fortunately, the museum was spared and later restored for the park's 100th anniversary in 1985. While the exhibits still provide visitors with an insight into the intricate workings of various park ecosystems, they are also an interesting link to the park's past. Staff lead a guided tour through the facility daily through summer at 3 P.M. and Saturday–Sunday the rest of the year at 2:30 P.M. The museum also has a Discovery Room, where touching the displays is encouraged, and a reading room is stocked with books on the park.

Whyte Museum of the Canadian Rockies

◖ Whyte Museum of the Canadian Rockies

The Whyte Foundation was established in the mid-1950s by local artists Peter and Catharine Whyte to help preserve artistic and historical material relating to the Canadian Rockies. Their museum (111 Bear St., 403/762-2291, 10 A.M.–5 P.M. daily, adult $7, child free) opened in 1968 and has continued to grow ever since. It now houses the world's largest collection of Canadian Rockies literature and art. Included in the archives are more than 4,000 volumes, oral tapes of early pioneers and outfitters, antique postcards, old cameras, manuscripts, and a large photography collection. The highlight is the photography of Byron Harmon, whose black-and-white studies of mountain geography have shown people around the world the beauty of the Canadian Rockies. The downstairs gallery features changing art exhibitions. The museum also houses the library and archives of the Alpine Club of Canada. On the grounds are several heritage homes

formerly occupied by local pioneers, including Bill Peyto, and backcountry cabins used by wardens.

MUSEUM WALKING TOURS

The Whyte Museum hosts interesting walking tours through summer. The most popular of these is the **Historic Banff Walk,** which departs from the museum at 2:30 P.M. daily, taking around 90 minutes to traverse the historic parts of downtown; $8 per person. The **Heritage Homes Tour** allows an opportunity for visitors to take a closer look at the historic residences located in the trees behind the museum, including that of Peter and Catharine Whyte. This tour departs at 11 A.M. and 2:30 P.M. daily in summer and also costs $8 per person. Around 40 minutes is spent visiting the home of a prominent Banff family on the **Luxton Home & Garden Tour.** Departures are at 1 P.M. daily in summer only; $8.

Cascade Gardens

Across the river from downtown, Cascade

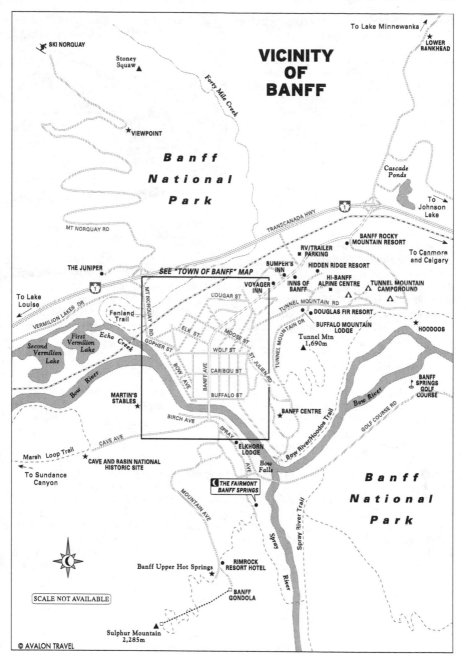

VICINITY
OF
BANFF

To Lake Minnewanka

SKI NORQUAY

LOWER
BANKHEAD

Stoney
Squaw

Forty Mile Creek

VIEWPOINT

Banff
National
Park

Cascade
Ponds

To
Johnson
Lake

MT NORQUAY RD

TRANSCANADA HWY

BANFF ROCKY
MOUNTAIN RESORT

THE JUNIPER

SEE "TOWN OF BANFF" MAP

RV/TRAILER
PARKING

BUMPER'S
INN

HIDDEN RIDGE RESORT

To Canmore
and Calgary

VOYAGER
INN

INNS OF
BANFF

HI-BANFF
ALPINE CENTRE

TUNNEL MOUNTAIN
CAMPGROUND

To Lake
Louise

COUGAR ST

TUNNEL MOUNTAIN RD

DOUGLAS FIR RESORT

VERMILION LAKES DR

Fenland
Trail

BUFFALO MOUNTAIN
LODGE

HOODOOS

First
Vermilion
Lake

Echo Creek

ELK ST

MOOSE ST

TUNNEL MOUNTAIN DR

Tunnel Mtn
1,690m

Second
Vermilion
Lake

GOPHER ST

WOLF ST

ST JULIEN RD

Bow River

BOW AVE

BANFF AVE

CARIBOU ST

BANFF
SPRINGS
GOLF
COURSE

MARTIN'S
STABLES

BUFFALO ST

BIRCH AVE

BANFF CENTRE

Bow River/Hoodoos Trail

Bow River

GOLF COURSE RD

SPRAY

Marsh Loop Trail

CAVE AVE

ELKHORN
LODGE

CAVE AND BASIN NATIONAL
HISTORIC SITE

Bow
Falls

Banff
National
Park

To Sundance
Canyon

MOUNTAIN AVE

THE FAIRMONT
BANFF SPRINGS

Spray River Trail

Spray

River

SCALE NOT AVAILABLE

Banff Upper Hot Springs

RIMROCK
RESORT HOTEL

BANFF
GONDOLA

© AVALON TRAVEL

Sulphur Mountain
2,285m

Gardens offers a commanding view along Banff Avenue and of Cascade Mountain. The gardens are immaculately manicured, making for enjoyable strolling on a sunny day. The stone edifice in the center of the garden is the **Park Administration Building** (101 Mountain Ave.), which dates to 1936. It replaced a private spa and hospital operated by one of the park's earliest entrepreneurs, Dr. R. G. Brett. Known as Brett's Sanatorium, the original 1886 structure was built to accommodate guests drawn to Banff by the claimed healing qualities of the hot springs' water.

Buffalo Nations Luxton Museum

Looking like a stockade, this museum (1 Birch Ave., 403/762-2388, 11 A.M.–6 P.M. daily in summer, 1–5 P.M. daily the rest of the year, adult $8, senior $6, child $2.50) overlooks the Bow River across from Central Park. It is dedicated to the heritage of the natives who once inhabited the Canadian Rockies and adjacent prairies. The museum was developed by prominent local resident Norman Luxton in the early 1900s. At that time it was within the Indian Trading Post, an adjacent gift shop that still stands. The museum contains memorabilia from Luxton's lifelong relationship with Stoney natives, including an elaborately decorated tepee, hunting equipment, arrowheads dating back 4,000 years, stuffed animals, original artwork, peace pipes, and traditional clothing. Various aspects of native culture—such as ceremonial gatherings, living in a tepee, and weaving—are also displayed. The Indian Trading Post is now one of Banff's better gift shops and is definitely worth a browse.

Cave and Basin National Historic Site

At the end of Cave Avenue, this historic site (403/762-1566, 9 A.M.–6 P.M. daily in summer, 11 A.M.–4 P.M. Mon.–Fri., 9:30 A.M.–5 P.M. Sat.–Sun. the rest of the year, adult $4, senior $3.50, child $2.50) is the birthplace of Banff National Park and of the Canadian National Parks system. Here in 1883, three

Cave and Basin National Historic Site

men employed by the CPR stumbled on the hot springs now known as the Cave and Basin and were soon lounging in the hot water—a real luxury in the Wild West. They built a fence around the springs, constructed a crude cabin, and began the long process of establishing a claim to the site. But the government beat them to it, settling their claims for a few thousand dollars and acquiring the hot springs.

Bathhouses were installed in 1887, and bathers paid $0.10 for a swim. The pools were eventually lined with concrete, and additions were built onto the original structures. Ironically, the soothing minerals in the water that had attracted millions of people to bathe here eventually caused the pools' demise. The minerals, combined with chlorine, produced sediments that ate away at the concrete structure until the pools were deemed unsafe. After closing in 1975, the pools were restored to their original look at a cost of $12 million. They reopened in 1985 only to close again in 1993 for the same reasons, coupled with flagging popularity.

Although the pools are now closed for swimming, the center is still one of Banff's most popular attractions. Interpretive displays describe the hows and whys of the springs. A narrow tunnel winds into the dimly lit cave, and short trails lead from the center to the cave entrance and through a unique environment created by the hot water from the springs. Interpretive tours run three times daily in summer.

Banff Upper Hot Springs

These springs (Mountain Ave., 403/762-1515, 9 A.M.–11 P.M. daily May–Oct., 10 A.M.–10 P.M. Sun.–Thurs. Oct.–May, 10 A.M.–11 P.M. Fri.–Sat. Oct.–May), toward the Banff Gondola, were first developed in 1901. The present building was completed in 1935, with extensive renovations made in 1996. Water flows out of the bedrock at 47°C (116.6°F) and is cooled to 40°C (104°F) in the main pool. Once considered for privatization, the springs are still run by Parks Canada and are popular throughout the year. Swimming is $7.50 adults, $6.50 seniors and children; lockers and towel rental are a couple of dollars extra. Within the complex is **Pleiades Massage & Spa** (403/760-2500), offering a wide range of therapeutic treatments, including massages from $55 for 30 minutes as well as body wraps, aromatherapy, and hydrotherapy.

Banff Gondola

The easiest way to get high above town without breaking a sweat is on this gondola (403/762-2523, 8:30 A.M.–9 P.M. daily in summer, shorter hours the rest of the year, closed for two weeks in January, adult $28, child $13.50). The modern four-person cars rise 700 meters (2,300 feet) in eight minutes to the summit of 2,285-meter (7,500-foot) **Sulphur Mountain.** From the observation deck at the upper terminal, the breathtaking view includes the town, Bow Valley, Cascade Mountain, Lake Minnewanka, and the Fairholme Range. Bighorn sheep often hang around below the upper terminal. The short **Vista Trail** leads along a ridge to a restored weather observatory. Between 1903 and 1931, long before the gondola was built, Norman Sanson was the meteorological observer who collected data at the station. During this period he made more than 1,000 ascents of Sulphur Mountain, all in the line of duty.

The **Summit Restaurant** (403/762-7486) serves up cafeteria-style food combined with priceless views. Above this eatery is the **Panorama Room** (403/762-7486, June–mid-Oct.), dishing up more of the same, but buffet-style, and the Chinese **Regal View Restaurant** (403/762-7486).

From downtown, the gondola is three kilometers (1.9 miles) along Mountain Avenue. May–October, **Brewster** (403/762-6767) provides shuttle service to the gondola from downtown hotels.

A 5.5-kilometer (3.4-mile) hiking trail to the summit begins from the Upper Hot Springs parking lot. Although it's a long slog, you'll be rewarded with a discounted gondola ride down ($10 one-way).

◖ The Fairmont Banff Springs

On a terrace above a bend in the Bow River is one of the largest, grandest, and most opulent mountain-resort hotels in the world. What better way to spend a rainy afternoon than to explore this turreted 20th-century castle (405 Spray Ave., 403/762-2211, www.fairmont.com/banff-springs), seeking out a writing desk overlooking one of the world's most-photographed scenes and penning a long letter to the folks back home?

"The Springs" has grown with the town and is an integral part of local history. William Cornelius Van Horne, vice president of the CPR, decided that the best way of encouraging customers to travel on his newly completed rail line across the Rockies was to build a series of luxurious mountain accommodations. The largest of these was begun in 1886, as close as possible to Banff's newly discovered hot springs. The location chosen had magnificent views and was only a short carriage ride from the train station. Money was no object, and architect Bruce Price began designing a mountain resort the likes of which the world had never seen. At some stage of construction his plans were misinterpreted, and much to Van Horne's shock, the building was built back to front. The best guest rooms faced the forested slopes of Sulphur Mountain while the kitchen had panoramic views of the Bow Valley.

© ANDREW HEMPSTEAD

The Bow River flows through the heart of Banff.

On June 1, 1888, it opened, the largest hotel in the world, with 250 rooms beginning at $3.50 per night including meals. Water from the nearby hot springs was piped into the hotel's steam baths. Rumor has it that when the pipes blocked, water from the Bow River was used, secretly supplemented by bags of sulphur-smelling chemicals. Overnight, the quiet community of Banff became a destination resort for wealthy guests from around the world, and the hotel soon became one of North America's most popular accommodations. Every room was booked every day during the short summer seasons. In 1903, a wing was added, doubling the hotel's capacity. The following year a tower was added to each wing. Guest numbers reached 22,000 in 1911, and construction of a new hotel, designed by Walter Painter, began that year. The original design—an 11-story tower joining two wings in a baronial style—was reminiscent of a Scottish castle mixed with a French country château. This concrete-and-rock-faced, green-roofed building stood as it did at its completion in 1928 until 1999, when an ambitious multiyear program of renovations commenced. At first, the most obvious change to those who have visited before is the new lobby, moved to a more accessible location, but all rooms have also been refurbished, and many of the restaurants changed or upgraded. The Canadian Pacific moniker remained part of the Banff Spring's official name until 2000, when the hotel, and all other Canadian Pacific hotels, became part of the Fairmont Hotels and Resorts chain.

Don't let the hotel's opulence keep you from spending time here. Wander through, admiring the 5,000 pieces of furniture and antiques (most of those in public areas are reproductions), paintings, prints, tapestries, and rugs. Take in the medieval atmosphere of Mount Stephen Hall, with its lime flagstone floor, enormous windows, and large oak beams; take advantage of the luxurious spa facility; or relax in one of 12 eateries or four lounges.

The hotel is a 15-minute walk southeast of town, either along Spray Avenue or via the trail along the south bank of the Bow River. **Banff Transit** buses leave Banff Avenue for the Springs twice an hour; $2. Alternatively, horse-drawn buggies take passengers from the Trail Rider Store (132 Banff Ave., 403/762-4551) to the Springs for about $90 for two passengers.

Bow Falls

Small but spectacular Bow Falls is below the Fairmont Banff Springs, only a short walk from downtown. The waterfall is the result of a dramatic change in the course of the Bow River brought about by glaciation. At one time the river flowed north of Tunnel Mountain and out of the mountains via the valley of Lake Minnewanka. As the glaciers retreated, they left terminal moraines, forming natural dams and changing the course of the river. Eventually the backed-up water found an outlet here between Tunnel Mountain and the northwest ridge of Mount Rundle. The falls are most spectacular in late spring when runoff from the winter snows fills every river and stream in the Bow Valley watershed.

To get there from town, cross the bridge at the south end of Banff Avenue, scramble down the grassy embankment to the left, and follow

© ANDREW HEMPSTEAD

The Fairmont Banff Springs, one of the world's great mountain resorts

a pleasant trail along the Bow River to a point above the falls. This easy walk is one kilometer (0.6 mile); 20 minutes each way. By car, cross the bridge and follow Golf Course signs. From the falls a paved road crosses the Spray River and passes through the golf course.

Banff Centre

On the lower slopes of Tunnel Mountain is Banff Centre, whose surroundings provide inspiration as one of Canada's leading centers for postgraduate students in a variety of disciplines, including Mountain Culture, Arts, and Leadership Development. The Banff Centre opened in the summer of 1933 as a theater school. Since then it has grown to become a prestigious institution attracting artists of many disciplines from throughout Canada. The Centre's **Walter Phillips Gallery** (St. Julien Rd., 403/762-6281, 12:30–5 P.M. Wed.–Sun.) presents changing exhibits of visual arts from throughout the world.

Activities are held on the grounds of the Banff Centre year-round. Highlights include a summer educational program, concerts, displays, live performances, the Playbill Series,

the Banff Arts Festival, and Banff Mountain Festivals, to name a few. Call 403/762-6100 for a program, go to the website www.banffcentre. ca, or check the *Crag and Canyon* (published weekly on Tuesday).

Vermilion Lakes

This series of shallow lakes forms an expansive montane wetland supporting a variety of mammals and 238 species of birds. Vermilion Lakes Drive, paralleling the TransCanada Highway immediately west of Banff, provides the easiest access to the area. The level of **First Vermilion Lake** was once controlled by a dam. Since its removal, the level of the lake has dropped. This is the beginning of a long process that will eventually see the area evolve into a floodplain forest such as is found along the Fenland Trail. **Second** and **Third Vermilion Lakes** have a higher water level that is controlled naturally by beaver dams. Near First Vermilion Lake is an active osprey nest. The entire area is excellent for wildlife viewing, especially in winter when it provides habitat for elk, coyote, and the occasional wolf.

© ANDREW HEMPSTEAD

Vermilion Lakes and Mount Rundle

Mount Norquay Road

One of the best views of town accessible by vehicle is on this road, which switchbacks steeply to the base of Ski Norquay, the local hangout for skiers and boarders. On the way up are several lookouts, including one near the top where bighorn sheep often graze.

To Lake Minnewanka

Lake Minnewanka Road begins where Banff Avenue ends at the northeast end of town. An alternative to driving along Banff Avenue is to take Buffalo Street, opposite the Banff Park Museum, and follow it around Tunnel Mountain, passing the campground and several viewpoints of the north face of Mount Rundle, rising vertically from the forested valley. This road eventually rejoins Banff Avenue at the Banff Rocky Mountain Resort.

After passing under the TransCanada Highway, **Cascade Falls** is obvious off to the left beyond the airstrip. The base of the falls can be easily reached in five minutes (climbing higher without the proper equipment is dangerous). In winter, these falls freeze, and you'll often see ice climbers slowly making

their way up the narrow thread of frozen water. Directly opposite is a turn to **Cascade Ponds,** a popular day-use area where families gather on warmer days to swim, sunbathe, and barbecue.

The next turnout along this road is at **Lower Bankhead.** During the early 1900s, Bankhead was a booming mining town producing 200,000 tons of coal a year. The poor quality of coal and bitter labor disputes led to the mine's closure in 1922. Soon after, all the buildings were moved or demolished. Although for many years the mine had brought prosperity to the park, perceptions changed. The National Parks Act of 1930, which prohibited the establishment of mining claims in national parks, was greeted with little animosity.

From the parking lot at Lower Bankhead, a 1.1-kilometer (0.7-mile) interpretive trail leads through the industrial section of the town and past an old mine train. The town's 1,000 residents lived on the other side of the road at what is now known as **Upper Bankhead.** Just before the Upper Bankhead turnoff, the foundation of the Holy Trinity Church can be seen on the side of the hill to the right. Not much remains of Upper Bankhead. It is now a day-use area with picnic tables, kitchen shelters, and firewood. Through the meadow to the west of here are some large slag heaps, concealed mine entrances, and various stone foundations.

Lake Minnewanka

Minnewanka (Lake of the Water Spirit) is the largest body of water in Banff National Park. Mount Inglismaldie (2,964 meters/9,720 feet) and the Fairholme Range form an imposing backdrop. The reservoir was first constructed in 1912, and additional dams were built in 1922 and 1941 to supply hydroelectric power to Banff. Even if you don't feel up to an energetic hike, it's worth parking at the facility area and going for a short walk along the lakeshore. You'll pass a concession selling snacks and drinks, then the tour boat dock, before entering an area of picnic tables and covered cooking shelters—the perfect place for a picnic. Children will love exploring the rocky shoreline and stony beaches in this area, but you should continue farther around the lake, if only to escape the crowds.

Minnewanka Lake Cruise (403/762-3473) is a 90-minute cruise to the far reaches of the lake, passing the Devil's Gap formation. It departs from the dock late May to early October 3–5 times daily (first sailing is 10:30 A.M. and costs adult $44, child $19). Brewster (403/762-6767) offers this cruise combined with a bus tour from Banff for $64. Easy walking trails lead along the western shore. The lake is great for fishing (lake trout to 15 kilograms/33 pounds) and is the only one in the park where motorboats are allowed. The same company operating the tour boats rents aluminum boats with small outboard engines.

From Lake Minnewanka the road continues along the reservoir wall, passing a plaque commemorating the Palliser Expedition. You'll often have to slow down along this stretch of road for bighorn sheep. The road then descends to **Two Jack Lake** and a small day-use area. Take the turnoff to **Johnson Lake,** to

access a lakeside trail, good swimming, and picnic facilities with views across to Mount Rundle.

◖ Bow Valley Parkway

Two roads link Banff to Lake Louise. The TransCanada Highway is the quicker route, more popular with through traffic. The other is the more scenic 51-kilometer (32-mile) Bow Valley Parkway, which branches off the TransCanada Highway five kilometers (3.1 miles) west of Banff. Cyclists will appreciate this road's two long, divided sections and low speed limit (60 kph/37 mph). Along this route are several impressive viewpoints, interpretive displays, picnic areas, good hiking, great opportunities for viewing wildlife, a hostel, three lodges, campgrounds, and one of the park's best restaurants. Between March and late June, the southern end of the parkway (as far north as Johnston Canyon) is closed 6 P.M.–9 A.M. daily for the protection of wildlife.

As you enter the parkway, you pass the quiet, creekside **Fireside** picnic area, where an interpretive display describes how the Bow Valley

© ANDREW HEMPSTEAD

Cycling is a good way to explore the Bow Valley Parkway.

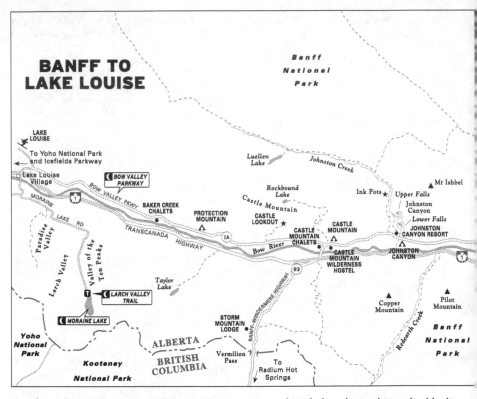

was formed. At **Backswamp Viewpoint,** you can look upstream to the site of a former dam, now a swampy wetland filled with aquatic vegetation. Farther along the road is another wetland at **Muleshoe.** This wetland consists of oxbow lakes that were formed when the Bow River changed its course and abandoned its meanders for a more direct path. Across the parkway is a one-kilometer (0.6-mile) trail that climbs to a viewpoint overlooking the valley. (The slope around this trail is infested with wood ticks during late spring/early summer, so be sure to check yourself carefully after hiking in this area.) To the east, **Hole-in-the-Wall** is visible. This large-mouthed cave was created by the Bow Glacier, which once filled the valley. As the glacier receded, its meltwater dissolved the soft limestone bedrock, creating what is known as a solution cave.

Beyond Muleshoe the road inexplicably divides for a few car lengths. A large white spruce stood on the island until it blew down in 1984. The story goes that while the road was being constructed, a surly foreman was asleep in the shade of the tree, and not daring to rouse him, workers cleared the roadway around him. The road then passes through particularly hilly terrain, part of a massive rock slide that occurred approximately 8,000 years ago.

Continuing down the parkway, you'll pass the following sights.

JOHNSTON CANYON
Johnston Creek drops over a series of spectacular waterfalls here, deep within the chasm it has carved into the limestone bedrock. The canyon is not nearly as deep as Maligne Canyon in Jasper National Park—30 meters (100 feet) at

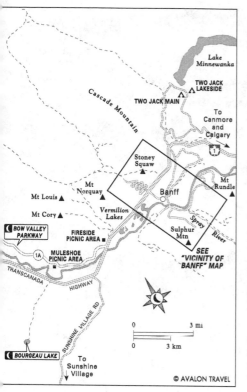

Lake Minnewanka

TWO JACK LAKESIDE

TWO JACK MAIN

Cascade Mountain

To Canmore and Calgary

Stoney Squaw

Mt Norquay

Mt Louis

Mt Cory

Banff

Mt Rundle

Vermilion Lakes

Spray River

BOW VALLEY PARKWAY

FIRESIDE PICNIC AREA

Sulphur Mtn

MULESHOE PICNIC AREA

SEE "VICINITY OF BANFF" MAP

TRANSCANADA

HIGHWAY

SUNSHINE VILLAGE RD

BOURGEAU LAKE

To Sunshine Village

0   3 mi
0   3 km

© AVALON TRAVEL

The city was founded by John Healy, who also founded the notorious Fort Whoop-Up in Lethbridge. During its heady days, five mines were operating, extracting not silver but ore rich in copper and lead. The town had a half dozen hotels, four or five stores, two real-estate offices, and a station on the transcontinental rail line when its demise began. Two men, named Patton and Pettigrew, salted their mine with gold and silver ore to attract investors. After selling 2,000 shares at $5 each, they vanished, leaving investors with a useless mine. Investment in the town ceased, mines closed, and the people left. Only one man refused to leave. His name was James Smith, but he was known to everyone as Joe. In 1887, when Silver City came under the jurisdiction of the National Parks Service, Joe was allowed to remain. He did so and was friendly to everyone, including Stoney natives, Father Albert Lacombe (who occasionally stopped by), well-known Banff guide Tom Wilson, and of course the animals who grazed around his cabin. By 1926, he was unable to trap or hunt due to failing eyesight, and many people tried to persuade him to leave. It wasn't until 1937 that he finally moved to a Calgary retirement home, where he died soon after.

its deepest, compared to 50 meters (165 feet) at Maligne—but the catwalk that leads to the lower falls has been built through the depths of the canyon rather than along its lip, making it seem just as spectacular. The lower falls are one kilometer (0.6 mile) from Johnston Canyon Resort, while the equally spectacular upper falls are a further 1.6 kilometers (one mile) upstream. Beyond this point are the **Ink Pots,** mineral springs whose sediments reflect sunlight, producing a brilliant aqua color. While in the canyon, look for nesting great gray owls and black swifts.

SILVER CITY
At the west end of **Moose Meadows,** a small plaque marks the site of Silver City. At its peak, this boomtown had a population of 2,000, making it bigger than Calgary at the time.

CASTLE MOUNTAIN TO LAKE LOUISE
After you leave the former site of Silver City, the aptly named Castle Mountain comes into view. It's one of the park's most recognizable peaks and most interesting geographical features. The mountain consists of very old rock (approximately 500 million years old) sitting atop much younger rock (a mere 200 million years old). This unusual situation occurred as the mountains were forced upward by pressure below the earth's surface, thrusting the older rock up and over the younger rock in places.

The road skirts the base of the mountain, passes Castle Mountain Village (which has gas, food, and accommodations), and climbs a small hill to Storm Mountain Viewpoint, which provides more stunning views and a picnic area. The next commercial facility is **Baker Creek Chalets and Bistro** (403/522-2182), an

Johnston Canyon

excellent spot for a meal. Then it's on to another viewpoint at Morant's Curve, from where Temple Mountain is visible. After passing another picnic area and a chunk of Precambrian shield, the road rejoins the TransCanada Highway at Lake Louise.

HIKING

After experiencing the international thrills of Banff Avenue, most people will want to see the *real* park, which is, after all, the reason that millions of visitors flock here, thousands take low-paying jobs just to stay here, and others become so severely addicted that they start families and live happily ever after here.

Although many landmarks can be seen from the roadside, to really experience the park's personality you'll need to go for a hike. One of the best things about Banff's 80-odd hiking trails is the variety. From short interpretive walks originating in town to easy hikes rewarded by spectacular vistas to myriad overnight backcountry opportunities, Banff's trails offer something for everyone.

Before attempting any hikes, visit the **Banff Visitor Centre** (224 Banff Ave., 403/762-1550), where staff can advise you on the condition of trails and closures. The best book on hiking in the park is the *Canadian Rockies Trail Guide*, which covers each trail in exacting detail.

If you are planning an overnight trip into the backcountry, you *must* pick up a backcountry camping pass from either of the park information centers before heading out; $10 per person per night or $70 for an annual pass.

Fenland

- Length: 2 kilometers/1.2 miles (30 minutes) round-trip
- Elevation gain: none
- Rating: easy
- Trailhead: Forty Mile Creek Picnic Area, Mount Norquay Road, 300 meters (0.2 mile) north of the rail crossing

If you've just arrived in town, this short

interpretive trail provides an excellent introduction to the Bow Valley ecosystem. A brochure, available at the trailhead, explains the various stages in the transition between wetland and floodplain spruce forest, visible as you progress around the loop. This fen environment is prime habitat for many species of birds. The work of beavers can be seen along the trail, and elk are here during winter. This trail is also a popular shortcut for joggers and cyclists heading for Vermilion Lakes.

Tunnel Mountain

*   Length: 2.3 kilometers/1.4 miles (30–60 minutes) one-way
*   Elevation gain: 300 meters/990 feet
*   Rating: easy/moderate
*   Trailhead: St. Julien Road, 350 meters (0.2 mile) south of Wolf Street

Accessible from town, this short hike is an easy climb to one of the park's lower peaks. It ascends the western flank of Tunnel Mountain

through a forest of lodgepole pine, switchbacking past some viewpoints before reaching a ridge just below the summit. Here the trail turns northward, climbing through a forest of Douglas fir to the summit (which is partially treed, preventing 360-degree views).

Bow River/Hoodoos

*   Length: 4.8 kilometers/3 miles (60–90 minutes) one-way
*   Elevation gain: minimal
*   Rating: easy
*   Trailhead: Bow River Viewpoint, Tunnel Mountain Drive

From a viewpoint famous for the Fairmont Banff Springs outlook, the trail descends to the Bow River, passing under the sheer east face of Tunnel Mountain. It then follows the river a short distance before climbing into a meadow where deer and elk often graze. From this perspective the north face of Mount Rundle is particularly imposing. As the trail climbs you'll hear

© ANDREW HEMPSTEAD

walking along the Bow River

the traffic on Tunnel Mountain Road long before you see it. The trail ends at hoodoos, strange limestone-and-gravel columns jutting mysteriously out of the forest. An alternative to returning the same way is to catch the Banff Transit bus from Tunnel Mountain Campgrounds. It leaves every half hour; the trip costs $2.

Sundance Canyon

- Length: 4.4 kilometers/2.7 miles (90 minutes) one-way
- Elevation gain: 100 meters/330 feet
- Rating: easy
- Trailhead: Cave and Basin National Historic Site

Sundance Canyon is a rewarding destination across the river from downtown. Unfortunately, the first three kilometers (1.9 miles) are along a paved road that is closed to traffic (but not bikes) and hard on your soles. Occasional glimpses of the Sawback Range are afforded by breaks in the forest. Where the paved road ends, the 2.4-kilometer (1.5-mile) Sundance Loop begins. Sundance Creek was once a larger river whose upper drainage basin was diverted by glacial action. Its powerful waters have eroded into the soft bedrock, forming a spectacular overhanging canyon whose bed is strewn with large boulders that have tumbled in.

Spray River

- Length: 6 kilometers/3.7 miles (2 hours) one-way
- Elevation gain: 70 meters/230 feet

SUNSHINE MEADOWS

Sunshine Meadows, straddling the Continental Divide, is a unique and beautiful region of the Canadian Rockies. It's best known as home to Sunshine Village, a self-contained alpine resort accessible only by gondola from the valley floor. But for a few short months each summer, the area is clear of snow and becomes a wonderland for hiking. Large amounts of precipitation create a lush cover of vegetation – over 300 species of wildflowers alone have been recorded here.

From Sunshine Village, trails radiate across the alpine meadow, which is covered in a colorful carpet of fireweed, glacier lilies, mountain avens, white mountain heather, and forget-me-nots (the meadows are in full bloom late July-mid-August). The most popular destination is **Rock Isle Lake,** an easy 2.5-kilometer (1.6-mile) jaunt from the upper village that crosses the Continental Divide while only gaining 100 meters (330 feet) of elevation. Mount Assiniboine (3,618 meters/11,870 feet), known as the "Matterhorn of the Rockies," is easily distinguished to the southeast. Various viewpoints punctuate the descent to an observation point overlooking the lake. From here, options include a loop around Larix Lake and a traverse along Standish Ridge. If the weather is cooperating, it won't matter which direction you head (so long as it's along a formed trail); you'll experience the Canadian Rockies in all their glory.

It's possible to walk the six-kilometer (3.7-mile) restricted-access road up to the meadows, but a more practical alternative is to take the Sunshine Meadows Alpine Shuttle along a road closed to public traffic. This service is operated by **White Mountain Adventures** (403/762-7889 or 800/408-0005, www.sunshinemeadowsbanff.com). Through a June-September season, buses depart Banff (at 8:30 A.M. daily, adult $55, child $30 round-trip) and the Sunshine Village parking lot (on the hour 9 A.M.-5 P.M. daily, adult $25, child $15 round-trip). The shuttle returns from the alpine meadow 2:30-5:30 P.M., with the 2:30 P.M. and 5:30 P.M. departures continuing to Banff. For $35 extra, you can explore the meadows with a naturalist, who will lead you through all the highlights. Advance reservations are required for both the bus and guided hike. To get to the base of the gondola from Banff, follow the TransCanada Highway nine kilometers (5.6 miles) west to Sunshine Village Road, which continues a similar distance along Healy Creek to the Sunshine Village parking lot.

- Rating: easy/moderate
- Trailhead: From the Bow Falls parking lot, cross the Spray River and walk along Golf Course Road to behind the green of the first golf hole on the right-hand side of the road.

This trail follows one of the many fire roads in the park. It is not particularly interesting, but it's accessible from downtown Banff and makes a pleasant way to escape the crowds. From behind the green of the 15th hole on the Stanley Thompson 18, the trail heads uphill into the forest. It follows the Spray River closely—when not in sight, the river can always be heard. For those so inclined, a river crossing one kilometer (0.6 mile) from the golf course allows for a shorter loop. Continuing south, the trail climbs a bluff for a good view of the Fairmont Banff Springs and Bow Valley. The return journey is straightforward with occasional views, ending at a locked gate behind the Fairmont Banff Springs, a short walk to Bow Falls.

For serious hikers this trail provides access to the park's rugged and remote southern reaches, but there's another interesting option involving this trail for eager day hikers. It involves arranging a lift to the trailhead of the Goat Creek hike in Spray Valley Provincial Park in Kananaskis Country. From this trailhead, it's 19 kilometers/11.8 miles (six hours) one-way back to Banff down the Spray River watershed on a trail that drops 370 meters (1,210 feet) in elevation. The trail is most popular with mountain bikers and cross-country skiers.

Western Slope of Mount Rundle

- Length: 5.4 kilometers/3.3 miles (2 hours) one-way
- Elevation gain: 480 meters/1,755 feet
- Rating: moderate
- Trailhead: From the Bow Falls parking lot, cross the Spray River and walk along Golf Course Road to behind the green of the first golf hole on the right-hand side of the road.

At 2,950 meters (9,680 feet), Mount Rundle is one of the park's dominant peaks. Climbing to its summit is possible without ropes, but previous scrambling experience is advised. An alternative is to ascend the mountain's western slope along an easy-to-follow trail that ends just over 1,000 vertical meters (3,280 vertical feet) before the summit. The trail follows the Spray River Trail from Golf Course Road, branching off left after 700 meters (0.4 mile). Climbing steadily, it breaks out of the enclosed forest after 2.5 kilometers (1.6 miles). The trail ends in a gully from which the undefined route to the summit begins.

Stoney Squaw

- Length: 2.4-kilometer/1.5-mile loop (1 hour round-trip)
- Elevation gain: 180 meters/590 feet
- Rating: easy
- Trailhead: top of Mount Norquay Road, 6 kilometers (3.7 miles) from town

Looking north along Banff Avenue, Stoney Squaw's 1,884-meter (6,180-foot) summit is dwarfed by Cascade Mountain, directly behind it. To get to the trailhead of a trail that leads to its easily reached summit, follow Mount Norquay Road to a parking lot in front of the resort's day lodge. Immediately to the right of the entrance, a small sign marks the trail. The narrow, slightly overgrown trail passes through a thick forest of lodgepole pine and spruce before breaking out into the open near the summit. The sweeping panorama includes Vermilion Lakes, the Bow Valley, Banff, Spray River Valley, Mount Rundle, Lake Minnewanka, and the imposing face of Cascade Mountain (2,998 meters/9,840 feet). The return trail follows the northwest slope of Stoney Squaw to an old ski run at the opposite end of the parking lot.

Cascade Amphitheatre

- Length: 6.6 kilometers/4.1 miles (2–3 hours) one-way

- Elevation gain: 610 meters/2,000 feet
- Rating: moderate/difficult
- Trailhead: day lodge, top of Mount Norquay Road, 6 kilometers (3.7 miles) from town

This enormous cirque and the subalpine meadows directly behind Cascade Mountain are one of the most rewarding destinations for hiking in the Banff area. The demanding trail begins by passing the day lodge, then skirting the base of several lifts, and following an old road to the floor of Forty Mile Valley. Keep right at all trail junctions. One kilometer (0.6 mile) after crossing Forty Mile Creek, the trail begins switchbacking up the western flank of Cascade Mountain through a forest of lodgepole pine. Along the way are breathtaking views of Mount Louis's sheer east face. After the trail levels off, it enters a magnificent U-shaped valley, and the amphitheater begins to define itself. The trail becomes indistinct in the subalpine meadow, which is carpeted in colorful wildflowers during summer. Farther up the valley, vegetation thins out as boulderstrewn talus slopes cover the ground. If you sit still long enough on these rocks, marmots and pikas will slowly appear, emitting shrill whistles before disappearing again.

The most popular route to the summit of 2,998-meter (9,840-foot) Cascade Mountain is along the southern ridge of the amphitheater wall. It is a long scramble up scree slopes and is made more difficult by a false summit; it should be attempted only by experienced scramblers.

C Level Cirque   *Trisha*

- Length: 4 kilometers/2.5 miles (90 minutes) one-way
- Elevation gain: 455 meters/1,500 feet
- Rating: moderate
- Trailhead: Upper Bankhead Picnic Area, Lake Minnewanka Road, 3.5 kilometers (2.2 miles) beyond the TransCanada Highway underpass

From a picnic area that sits on the site of an abandoned mining town, the trail climbs steadily through a forest of lodgepole pine, aspen, and spruce to a pile of tailings and broken-down concrete walls. Soon after is a panoramic view of Lake Minnewanka, then the trail reenters the forest before ending in a small cirque with views down the Bow Valley to Canmore and beyond. The cirque is carved into the eastern face of Cascade Mountain, where snow often lingers until July. When the snow melts, the lush soil is covered in a carpet of colorful wildflowers.

Aylmer Lookout

- Length: 12 kilometers/7.5 miles (4 hours) one-way
- Elevation gain: 810 meters/2,660 feet
- Rating: moderate/difficult
- Trailhead: Lake Minnewanka, Lake Minnewanka Road, 5.5 kilometers (3.4 miles) beyond the TransCanada Highway underpass

The first eight-kilometer (five-mile) stretch of this trail follows the northern shore of Lake Minnewanka from the day-use area to a junction. The right fork leads to a campground, while the left climbs steeply to the site of an old fire tower on top of an exposed ridge. The deep blue waters of Lake Minnewanka are visible, backed by the imposing peaks of Mount Girouard (2,995 meters/9,830 feet) and Mount Inglismaldie (2,964 meters/9,725 feet). Bighorn sheep often graze in this area. From here a trail forks left and continues climbing to the alpine tundra of Aylmer Pass. (This trail is often closed in summer due to wildlife activity—check at the visitors center before heading out.)

Cory Pass

- Length: 5.8 kilometers/3.6 miles (2.5 hours) one-way
- Elevation gain: 920 meters/3,020 feet
- Rating: moderate/difficult
- Trailhead: Fireside Picnic Area, Banff end of the Bow Valley Parkway

This strenuous hike has a rewarding objective—a magnificent view of dog-toothed Mount Louis. The towering slab of limestone rises more than 500 meters (1,640 feet) from the valley below. Just over one kilometer (0.6 mile) from the trailhead, the trail divides. The left fork climbs steeply across an open slope to an uneven ridge that it follows before ascending yet another steep slope to Cory Pass—a wild, windy, desolate area surrounded in jagged peaks dominated by Mount Louis. An alternative to returning along the same trail is continuing down into Gargoyle Valley, following the base of Mount Edith before ascending to Edith Pass and returning to the junction one kilometer (0.6 mile) from the picnic area. Total distance for this trip is 13 kilometers (eight miles), a long day considering the steep climbs and descents involved.

Bourgeau Lake

* Length: 7.6 kilometers/4.7 miles (2.5 hours) one-way
* Elevation gain: 730 meters/2,400 feet
* Rating: moderate
* Trailhead: signposted parking lot, Trans Canada Highway, 3 kilometers (1.9 miles) west of Sunshine Village Junction

This trail follows Wolverine Creek to a small subalpine lake nestled at the base of an impressive limestone amphitheater. Although the trail is moderately steep, plenty of distractions along the way are worthy of a stop (and rest). Back across the Bow Valley, the Sawback Range is easy to distinguish. As the forest of lodgepole pine turns to spruce, the trail passes under the cliffs of Mount Bourgeau and crosses Wolverine Creek (below a spot where it tumbles photogenically over exposed bedrock). After strenuous switchbacks, the trail climbs into the cirque containing Bourgeau Lake. As you explore the lake's rocky shore, you'll hear the colonies of noisy pikas, even if you don't see them.

Shadow Lake

* Length: 14.3 kilometers/8.9 miles (4.5 hours) one-way
* Elevation gain: 440 meters/1,445 feet
* Rating: moderate
* Trailhead: Redearth Creek Parking Area, TransCanada Highway, 11 kilometers (6.8 miles) west of Sunshine Village Junction

Shadow is one of the many impressive subalpine lakes along the Continental Divide and a popular base for a great variety of day trips. It follows the old Redearth fire road for 11 kilometers (6.8 miles) before forking right and climbing into the forest. The campground is two kilometers (1.2 miles) beyond this junction, and just 500 meters (0.3 mile) farther is **Shadow Lake Lodge.** The lake is nearly two kilometers (1.2 miles) long, and from its southern shore trails lead to Ball Pass, Gibbon Pass, and Haiduk Lake.

Castle Lookout

* Length: 3.7 kilometers/2.3 miles (90 minutes) one-way
* Elevation gain: 520 meters/1,700 feet
* Rating: moderate
* Trailhead: Bow Valley Parkway, 5 kilometers (3.1 miles) northwest of Castle Junction

However you travel through the Bow Valley, you can't help but be impressed by Castle Mountain rising proudly from the forest floor. This trail takes you above the tree line on the mountain's west face to the site of Mount Eisenhower fire lookout, abandoned in the 1970s and burned in the 1980s. From the Bow Valley Parkway, the trail follows a wide pathway for 1.5 kilometers (0.9 mile) to an abandoned cabin in a forest of lodgepole pine and spruce. It then becomes narrower and steeper, switchbacking through a meadow before climbing through a narrow band of rock and leveling off near the lookout site. Magnificent panoramas of the Bow Valley spread out before you in both directions. Storm Mountain can be seen directly across the valley.

Rockbound Lake

- Length: 8.4 kilometers/5.2 miles (2.5 hours) one-way
- Elevation gain: 760 meters/2,500 feet
- Rating: moderate/difficult
- Trailhead: Castle Junction, Bow Valley Parkway, 30 kilometers (18.6 miles) west of Banff

This strenuous hike leads to a delightful body of water tucked behind Castle Mountain. For the first five kilometers (3.1 miles) the trail follows an old fire road along the southern flanks of Castle Mountain. Early in the season or after heavy rain, this section can be boggy. Glimpses of surrounding peaks ease the pain of the steady climb as the trail narrows. After eight kilometers (five miles) you'll come to Tower Lake, which the trail skirts to the right before climbing a steep slope. From the top of the ridge, Rockbound Lake comes into view, and the reason for its name immediately becomes apparent. A scramble up any of the nearby slopes will reward you with good views.

MOUNTAIN BIKING

Whether you have your own bike or you rent one from the many bicycle shops in Banff or Lake Louise, cycling in the park is for everyone. The roads to Lake Minnewanka, Mount Norquay, through the golf course, and along the Bow Valley Parkway are all popular routes. Several trails radiating from Banff and ending deep in the backcountry have been designated as bicycle trails. These include Sundance (3.7 km/2.3 miles one-way), Rundle Riverside to Canmore (15 km/9.3 miles one-way), and the Spray River Loop (via Goat Creek; 48 km/30 miles round-trip). Farther afield, other trails are at Redearth Creek, Lake Louise, and in the northeastern reaches of the park near Saskatchewan River Crossing. Before heading into the backcountry, pick up the free *Mountain Biking and Cycling Guide* from the Banff or Lake Louise Visitor Centres. Riders are particularly susceptible to sudden bear

encounters. Be alert and make loud noises when passing through heavy vegetation.

Abominable (229 Wolf St., 403/762-5065), **Bactrax** (225 Bear St., 403/762-8177), **Banff Adventures Unlimited** (211 Bear St., 403/762-4554), and **Banff Springs Ski & Mountain Sports** (Fairmont Banff Springs, 405 Spray Ave., 403/762-5333), rent front- and full-suspension mountain bikes for $8–15 per hour and $35–60 per day. Rates include a helmet, lock, and biking map.

HORSEBACK RIDING

Jim and Bill Brewster led Banff's first paying guests into the backcountry on horseback more than 100 years ago. Today visitors are still able to enjoy the park on this traditional form of transportation.

Warner Guiding & Outfitting (www. horseback.com) offers a great variety of trips. Their main office is downtown in the **Trail Rider Store** (132 Banff Ave., 403/762-4551), although trips depart from either **Martin's**

One of the more popular horseback rides crosses the Spray River.

Stables (403/762-2832), behind the recreation grounds on Birch Avenue, or **Banff Springs Corral** (403/762-2848), along Spray Avenue. From Martin's Stables, the one-hour trip departs 9 A.M.–6 P.M. daily and takes in a pleasant circuit around the Marsh Loop ($40). A two-hour trip around the Sundance Loop ($72) departs four times daily. Other longer trips include the three-hour Mountain Morning Breakfast Ride, featuring a hearty breakfast along the trail (departs 9 A.M.; $102); Explorer Day Ride, a seven-hour ride up the lower slopes of Sulphur Mountain (departs 9 A.M.; $188); and the Evening Steak Fry, a three-hour ride with a suitably western steak and baked bean dinner along the trail (departs 5 P.M.; $102). For those not comfortable on horseback, the morning and evening trips come with the option to ride in a wagon (adult $82, child $72).

In addition to day trips, Warner runs a variety of overnight rides that include lodgings in backcountry lodges or tent camps. The main accommodation is Sundance Lodge, an easy 18-kilometer (10-mile) ride, which has 10 rooms, a large living area, and even hot showers. The shortest option is an overnight trip departing Saturday through summer for $553 per person. A three-day trip is $825. Four-day ($1,088) and five-day ($1,348) trips split their time between Sundance Lodge and Halfway Lodge, which is farther up the Spray Valley. Rates include horse rental, all meals, and accommodation.

WATER SPORTS
White-Water Rafting

Anyone looking for white-water-rafting action will want to run the **Kicking Horse River,** which flows down the western slopes of the Canadian Rockies into British Columbia. Many operators provide transportation from Banff and Lake Louise.

Rocky Mountain Raft Tours (403/762-3632) offers a one-hour (adult $42, child $21) float trip down the Bow River, beginning just below Bow Falls and ending along the golf

a raft tour on the Bow River

course loop road. The three-hour trip continues downriver to the park boundary (adult $84, child $42). No rapids are involved, so you'll stay dry.

Canoeing

On a quiet stretch of the Bow River, at the north end of Wolf Street, **Blue Canoe** (403/762-3632 or 403/760-5007; 9 A.M.–9 P.M. daily May–Sept.) rents canoes for use on the river, from where it's an easy paddle upstream to the Vermilion Lakes and Forty Mile Creek; $30 one hour, $45 two hours, or $65 for a full day of paddling.

Fishing and Boating

The finest fishing in the park is in Lake Minnewanka, where lake trout as large as 15 kilograms (33 pounds) have been caught. One way to ensure a good catch is through **Minnewanka Lake Cruise** (403/762-3473), which offers fishing trips in a heated cabin cruiser; trolling and downrigging are preferred methods of fishing the lake. A half-day's fishing (3.5 hours) is $356 for one or two persons. The company also rents small aluminum fishing boats with outboard motors for $42 for the first hour, then $15 for every extra hour to a maximum of $114 per day.

Before fishing anywhere in the park, you need a national park fishing license ($10 per day, $35 per year), available from the Banff and Lake Louise Visitor Centres and sport shops throughout the park.

GOLF

One of the world's most scenic golf courses, the **Banff Springs Golf Course** spreads out along the Bow River between Mount Rundle and Tunnel Mountain. The first course was laid out here in 1911, but in 1928 Stanley Thompson was brought in by the CPR to redesign it into 18 holes and to build what was at the time North America's most expensive course. In 1989, the Tunnel Nine opened (along with a new clubhouse), creating today's 27-hole course.

Between 1997 and 1999 no expense was spared in rebuilding the entire original 18 holes and adding longer tees, while also reverting to Thompson's planned sequence of play, known now as the **Stanley Thompson Classic.** The course is typically Thompson, taking advantage of natural contours and featuring elevated tees, wide fairways, treacherous fescue grass rough, and holes aligned to distant mountains. From the back markers it is 7,087 yards and plays to a par of 71. The course is not only breathtakingly beautiful, but it's also challenging for every level of golfer. Pick up a copy of the book *The World's Greatest Golf Holes,* and you'll see a picture of the fourth hole on the Rundle 9. It's a par three, over Devil's Cauldron 70 meters (230 feet) below, to a small green backed by the sheer face of Mount Rundle rising vertically more than 1,000 meters (3,280 feet) above the putting surface. Another unique feature of the course is the abundance of wildlife: There's always the chance of seeing elk feeding on fairways, or coyotes, deer, or black bears scurrying across.

Greens fees (including cart and driving range privileges) are $220, discounted to $125 in May and late September–early October. The Tunnel 9 offers the same spectacular challenges as Thompson's original layout but lacks the history; nine holes cost $80. Free shuttle buses run from the Fairmont Banff Springs to the clubhouse. (The original 1911 clubhouse still stands, but it has been replaced by a modern, circular building in the heart of the course.) There you'll find club rentals ($50–65), putting greens, a driving range, a pro shop, two chipping greens (one hidden up in the trees with surrounding bunkers), and a restaurant with a stunning wraparound deck. Booking tee times well in advance is essential; call 403/762-6801.

TOURS

Brewster (403/762-6767 or 877/791-5500, www.brewster.ca) is the dominant tour company in the area. The three-hour Discover Banff bus tour takes in downtown Banff, Tunnel Mountain Drive, the hoodoos, the Cave and Basin, and Banff Gondola (gondola

THE BREWSTER BOYS

Few guides in Banff were as well known as Jim and Bill Brewster. In 1892, at ages 10 and 12, respectively, they were hired by the Banff Springs Hotel to take guests to local landmarks. As their reputation as guides grew, they built a thriving business. By 1900, they had their own livery and outfitting company, and soon thereafter they expanded operations to Lake Louise. Their other early business interests included a trading post, the original Mt. Royal Hotel, the first ski lodge in the Sunshine Meadows, and the hotel at the Columbia Icefield.

Today, a legacy of the boys' savvy, Brewster, a transportation and tour company, has grown to become an integral part of many tourists' stays. The company operates some of the world's most advanced sightseeing vehicles, including a fleet of Ice Explorers on the Columbia Icefield.

fare included). This tour runs in summer only and departs from the bus depot at 8:30 A.M. daily; call for hotel pickup times. Adult fare is $78, children half price. Brewster also runs several other tours. A four-hour tour to Lake Louise departs select Banff hotels daily; $65. In winter this tour departs Tuesday and Friday mornings, runs five hours, and includes Banff sights; $65. During summer, the company also offers tours from Banff to Lake Minnewanka ($64; includes boat cruise), and Columbia Icefield ($149).

Discover Banff Tours (Sundance Mall, 215 Banff Ave., 403/760-5007 or 877/565-9372, www.bannftours.com) is a smaller company, with smaller buses and more personalized service. Its tour routes are similar to Brewster's: A three-hour Discover Banff tour visits Lake Minnewanka, the Cave and Basin, the Fairmont Banff Springs, and the hoodoos for adult $52, child $32; a full-day trip to the Columbia Icefield is adult $154, child

$79; and a two-hour Evening Wildlife Safari is adult $42, child $25. This company offers a good selection of other tours throughout the year, including a wintertime ice walk in frozen Johnston Canyon (adult $66, child $40).

WINTER RECREATION

From November till May, the entire park transforms itself into a winter playground covered in a blanket of snow. Of Alberta's six world-class winter resorts, three are in Banff National Park. Ski Norquay is a small but steep hill overlooking the town of Banff; Sunshine Village perches high in the mountains on the Continental Divide, catching more than its share of fluffy white powder; and Lake Louise, Canada's second-largest winter resort, spreads over four distinct mountain faces. Apart from an abundance of snow, the resorts have something else in common—spectacular views, which alone are worth the price of a lift ticket. Although the resorts operate independently, the **Ski Hub** (119 Banff Ave., 403/762-4754, www.skibig3.com; 7 A.M.–10 P.M. daily) represents all three and is the place to get information on multiday ticketing and transportation.

Other winter activities in the park include cross-country skiing, ice-skating, snowshoeing, dogsledding, and just relaxing. Crowds are nonexistent, and hotels reduce rates by up to 70 percent (except Christmas holidays)—reason enough to venture into the mountains. Lift and lodging packages begin at $80 per person.

Ski Norquay

Norquay (403/762-4421, www.banffnorquay.com) has two distinct faces—literally and figuratively. There are some great cruising runs and a well-respected ski school, but also the experts-only North American Chair (the one you can see from town), which opens up the famous double-black-diamond Upper Lone Pine run. Snowboarders congregate at a half pipe and terrain park. A magnificent post-and-beam day lodge nestled below the main runs is surrounded on one side by a wide deck that catches the afternoon sun, while holding a cafeteria, restaurant, and bar inside. Lift tickets are adult $65, youth and senior $55, child $25; lift, lesson, and rental packages cost about the same. Hourly passes provide some flexibility (two hours $30, three hours $40, etc). A few runs are lit for night skiing and boarding on Friday evening; adult $28, senior $26, child $15. A shuttle bus makes pickups from Banff hotels for the short, six-kilometer (3.7-mile) ride up to the resort; $8. The season at Norquay usually runs early December–early April.

Sunshine Village

Sunshine Village (403/762-6500 or 877/542-2633, www.skibanff.com) has lots going for it—more than six meters (20 feet) of snow annually (no need for snowmaking up here), wide-open bowls, a season stretching for nearly 200 days (mid-Nov.–late May), skiing and boarding in two provinces, and the only slopeside accommodations in the park.

The resort has grown up a lot in the last decade as high-speed quads have replaced old chairlifts and opened up new terrain such as Goat's Eye Mountain, and the original gondola was replaced by what is reputed to be the world's fastest gondola. One of Canada's most infamous runs, Delirium Dive, drops off the northeast-facing slope of Lookout Mountain; to ski or board this up-to-50-degree run, you must be equipped with a transceiver, shovel, probe, and partner, but you'll have bragging rights that night at the bar (especially if you've descended the Bre-X line). Aside from Delirium Dive, the area is best known for its excellent beginner and intermediate terrain, which covers 60 percent of the mountain. The total vertical rise is 1,070 meters (3,510 feet), and the longest run (down to the lower parking lot) is eight kilometers (five miles). Day passes are adult $78, senior $64, youth $58, child $31, and those younger than six ride free. Two days of lift access and one night's lodging at slopeside Sunshine Inn cost $220 per person in high season—an excellent deal. The inn has a restaurant, lounge, game room, and large outdoor hot tub. Transportation from Banff, Canmore, or Lake Louise to the resort is $12 round-trip;

check the website or inquire at major hotels for the timetable.

Rentals and Sales

Each resort has ski and snowboard rental and sales facilities, but getting your gear down in town is often easier. **Abominable Ski & Sportswear** (229 Banff Ave., 403/762-2905) and **Monod Sports** (129 Banff Ave., 403/762-4571) have been synonymous with Banff and the ski industry for decades, and while the **Rude Boys Snowboard Shop** (downstairs in the Sundance Mall, 215 Banff Ave., 403/762-8480) has only been around since the 1980s, it is *the* snowboarder hangout. Other shops with sales and rentals include **Banff Springs Ski & Mountain Sports** (Fairmont Banff Springs, 405 Spray Ave., 403/762-5333), **Mountain Magic Equipment** (224 Bear St., 403/762-2591), **Ski Hub** (119 Banff Ave., 403/762-4754), **Ski Stop** (203 Bear St., 403/760-1650), and **Snow Tips** (225 Bear St., 403/762-8177). Basic packages—skis, poles, and boots—are $30–40 per day, while high-performance packages range $45–60. Snowboards and boots rent for $35–60 per day.

Switching Gear (718 10th St., 403/678-1992), down the valley from Banff in nearby Canmore, has an excellent selection of used ski and snowboard equipment, as well as winter clothing at very reasonable prices.

Cross-Country Skiing

No better way of experiencing the park's winter delights exists than gliding through the landscape on cross-country skis. Many summer hiking trails are groomed for winter travel. The most popular areas near town are Johnson Lake, Golf Course Road, Spray River, Sundance Canyon, and upstream from the canoe docks. The booklet *Cross-country Skiing—Nordic Trails in Banff National Park* is available for $1 from the Banff Visitor Centre. Weather forecasts (403/762-2088) are posted at both centers.

Rental packages are available from **Snow Tips** (225 Bear St., 403/762-8177) and **Mountain Magic Equipment** (224 Bear St.,

AN ABRIDGED HISTORY OF SKIING IN BANFF NATIONAL PARK

Banff National Park is busiest during summer, but for many visitors from outside North America – especially Europeans and Australians – it is the winter season that they know Banff for. Regardless of its repute, and although winter (December–April) is considered low season, the park remains busy as ski enthusiasts from around the world gather for world-class skiing and boarding. It hasn't always been this way. As recently as the 1960s, many lodgings – including the famous Fairmont Banff Springs – were open only for the summer season.

With winter tourism nonexistent, the first skiers were Banff locals, who would climb local peaks under their own steam. Due mostly to its handy location close to town, a popular spot was **Mount Norquay,** which was skied as early as the 1920s. In 1948, Canada's first chairlift was installed on the mountain's eastern slopes. In the ensuing years, newer and faster lifts have created a convenient getaway that fulfills the needs of locals and visitors alike, who can buzz up for an afternoon of skiing or boarding on slopes that suit all levels of proficiency.

The first people to ski the **Sunshine Meadows** were two local men, Cliff White and Cyril Paris, who became lost in the spring of 1929 and returned to Banff with stories of deep snow and ideal slopes for skiing. In the following years, a primitive cabin was used as a base for overnight ski trips in the area. In 1938 the Canadian National Ski Championships were held here, and in 1942 a portable lift was constructed. The White family was synonymous with the Sunshine area for many years, running the lodge and ski area while Brewster buses negotiated the steep, narrow road that led to the meadows. In 1980 a gondola was installed to whisk skiers and snowboarders six kilometers (3.7 miles) from the valley floor to the alpine village.

The best known of Banff's three resorts is **Lake Louise,** an hour's drive north of town but still within park boundaries. This part of the park also attracted early interest from local skiers, beginning in 1930 when Cliff White and Cyril Paris built a small ski chalet in the Skoki Valley (now operating as Skoki Lodge). The remoteness of this hut turned out to be impractical, so another was built, closer to the road. In 1954, a crude lift was constructed up Larch Mountain from the chalet. The lift had only just begun operation when a young Englishman, Norman Watson (known as the "Barmy Baronet"), who had inherited a fortune, saw the potential for a world-class alpine resort and made the completion of his dream a lifelong obsession. Over the years more lifts were constructed, and two runs – Olympic Men's Downhill and Olympic Ladies' Downhill – were cut in anticipation of a successful bid for the 1968 Winter Olympics (the bid failed).

403/762-2591). Expect to pay $20–30 per day. **White Mountain Adventures** (403/678-4099 or 800/408-0005) offers lessons for $60 per person.

Ice-Skating

Skating rinks are located on the **Bow River** just up from Central Park and on the golf course side of the **Fairmont Banff Springs.** The latter rink is lit after dark, and a raging fire is built beside it—the perfect place to enjoy a hot chocolate. Early in the season (check conditions first), skating is possible on **Vermilion Lakes** and **Johnson Lake.** Rent skates from **Banff Springs Ski & Mountain Sports** (Fairmont Banff Springs, 405 Spray Ave., 403/762-5333) for $7 per hour.

Sleigh Rides

Warner Guiding and Outfitting offers sleigh rides ($32 per person) on the frozen Bow River throughout winter. For reservations, call 403/762-4551 or stop by the Trail Rider Store (132 Banff Ave.).

Ice Walks

Between December and late March, Johnston Canyon, a 20-minute drive from Banff along the Bow Valley Parkway, is a wonderland of frozen waterfalls. Two local companies, **Discover Banff Tours** (403/760-5007 or 877/565-9372) and **White Mountain Adventures** (403/678-4099 or 800/408-0005), offer ice walks through the canyon. Both tours reach as far as the Upper Falls and provide guests with ice cleats for their shoes and hot drinks to take the chill off this outdoor activity. Transportation in Banff is included in the rates of $65–70 per person.

Other Winter Activities

Beyond the skating rink below the Fairmont Banff Springs is an unofficial toboggan run; ask at your hotel for sleds or rent them from the sports store at the Fairmont Banff Springs; $6 per hour.

Go ice fishing December–April with **Banff Fishing Unlimited** (403/762-4936). Winter fishing is prohibited in Banff National Park, so this company will provide transportation to a heated hut on Spray Lake (Kananaskis Country) along with instruction in jigging for lake trout.

Anyone interested in **ice climbing** must register at the national park desk in the Banff Visitor Centre or call 403/762-1550. The world-famous (if you're an ice climber) Terminator is just outside the park boundary.

If none of these activities appeal to you, head to **Upper Hot Springs** (403/762-1515, 10 A.M.–10 P.M. daily, $7.50) for a relaxing soak.

Camping might not be everyone's idea of a winter holiday, but one section of **Tunnel Mountain Campground** remains open year-round.

INDOOR RECREATION
Swimming and Fitness Facilities

Many of Banff's bigger hotels have fitness rooms, and some have indoor pools. A popular place to swim and work out is in the **Sally Borden Fitness & Recreation Facility** (Banff Centre, St. Julien Rd., 403/762-6450, 6 A.M.–11 P.M. daily), which holds a wide range of fitness facilities, climbing gym, squash courts, a 25-meter-long heated pool, a wading pool, and a hot tub. General admission is $10.50, or pay $4.50 to swim only. Go to www. banffcentre.ca/sbb for a schedule.

Willow Stream Spa

This luxurious spa facility in the Fairmont Banff Springs (403/762-2211, 6 A.M.–10 P.M. daily) is the place to pamper yourself. Opened in 1995 at a cost of $12 million, it sprawls over two levels and 3,000 square meters (0.7 acre) of a private corner of the hotel. The epicenter of the facility is a circular mineral pool capped by a high glass-topped ceiling and ringed by floor-to-ceiling windows on one side and on the other by hot tubs fed by cascading waterfalls of varying temperatures. Other features include outdoor saltwater hot tubs, private solariums, steam rooms, luxurious bathrooms, a café featuring light meals, and separate male and female lounges complete with fireplaces and complimentary drinks and snacks. Numerous other services are offered, including facials, body wraps, massage therapy, salon services, and hydrotherapy. Entry to Willow Stream is included in some package rates for guests at the hotel. Admission is $80 per day for hotel guests, which includes the use of a locker and spa attire, with almost 100 services available at additional cost (most of these include general admission, so, for example, you can spend the day at Willow Stream and receive a one-hour massage for $185).

Other Indoor Recreation

Fairmont Banff Springs (403/762-2211) has a four-lane, five-pin bowling center; games are $5.25 per person. The **Lux Cinema Centre** (229 Bear St., 403/762-8595) screens new releases for $12 ($8 on Tuesday).

Banff's only waterslide is in the **Douglas Fir Resort** (Tunnel Mountain Dr., 403/762-5591, 4–9:30 P.M. Mon.–Fri., 10 A.M.–9:30 P.M. Sat.–Sun.). The two slides are indoors, and the admission price of $20 (free for kids younger than age five) includes use of a hot tub and exercise room.

NIGHTLIFE

Like resort towns around the world, Banff has a deserved reputation as a party town, especially among seasonal workers, the après-ski crowd, and young Calgarians. Crowds seem to spread out, with no particular bar being more popular than another or being a place where you can mingle with fellow travelers. Given the location and vacation vibe, drink prices are as high as you may expect, with attitude thrown in for free.

Banff is a nonsmoking town. Also note that the Royal Canadian Mounted Police (RCMP) patrol Banff all night, promptly arresting anyone who even looks like trouble, including anyone drunk or drinking on the streets.

Bars and Lounges

Wild Bill's (upstairs at 201 Banff Ave., 403/762-0333) is named for Banff guide Bill Peyto and is truly legendary. This frontier-style locale attracts the biggest and best bands of any Banff venue, with bookings that vary from local faves to washed-up rockers such as Nazareth; as a general rule, expect alternative music or underground country early in the week and better-known rock or pop Thursday–Sunday. Across the road, the **Maple Leaf** (137 Banff Ave., 403/760-7680) has a stylish space set aside as a bar. The **Elk & Oarsman** (119 Banff Ave., 403/762-4616) serves up beer and more in a clean, casual atmosphere that is as friendly as it gets in Banff. Across the road from Wild Bill's is the **Rose and Crown** (202 Banff Ave., 403/762-2121), serving British beers and hearty pub fare. It also features a rooftop patio and rock-and-roll bands a few nights a week, but there's not much room for dancing. Also down the main drag is **Tommy's** (120 Banff Ave., 403/762-8888), a perennial favorite for young seasonal workers and those who once were and now consider themselves as locals.

Around the corner from Banff Avenue, the **St. James Gate Olde Irish Pub** (207 Wolf St., 403/762-9355) is a large Irish-style bar with a reputation for excellent British-style meals and occasional appearances by Celtic bands.

One block back from Banff Avenue are two excellent choices for a quiet drink. Relative to other town drinking spots, prices at 🍺 **The Bison Restaurant and Lounge** (Bison Courtyard, Bear St., 403/762-5550) are excellent. Add funky surroundings and a sunny courtyard to the mix, and you have an excellent choice for a drink and meal. **Saltlik** (221 Bear St., 403/762-2467) is best known as an upscale (and upstairs) steakhouse. At street level, the lounge opens to a streetside patio.

Around the corner from these two choices is **Melissa's** (218 Lynx St., 403/762-5776), which is a longtime favorite drinking hole for locals. It has a small outdoor patio, a long evening happy hour, a pool table, and multiple TVs.

Hotel Hangouts

Many Banff hotels have lounges open to guests and nonguests alike. They are generally quieter than the bars listed previously and often offer abbreviated menus from adjacent restaurants. For old-world atmosphere, nothing in town comes close to matching the **Sir William Wallace Room,** in the Fairmont Banff Springs (403/762-2211, 4 P.M.–midnight daily). Another place to enjoy a drink in the park's landmark hotel is the mezzanine-level **Rundle Lounge** (Fairmont Banff Springs, 403/762-2211, noon–1 A.M. daily), an open space with views extending to the golf course. Below the hotel is the **Waldhaus Pub** (Fairmont Banff Springs, 403/762-2211; from 11 A.M. daily in summer). It has the best deck in town, but it's mainly the haunt of locals coming off the golf course or savvy visitors (such as those who've read this book).

Downtown, the **Mount Royal Hotel** (corner of Banff Ave. and Caribou St., 403/762-3331) has a small lounge off the lobby, while below, accessed from farther up Banff Avenue, is the **Buffalo Paddock** (138 Banff Ave., 403/762-3331), with pool tables. At the opposite end of the style scale is the lounge in the **Voyager Inn** (555 Banff Ave., 403/762-3301), which is worth listing for the fact that it has the cheapest beer in town and drink specials every night (and a liquor store with cheaper prices than downtown). Just past the Voyager Inn is

Bumpers (603 Banff Ave., 403/762-2622), a steakhouse with a small bar and pool table in a cozy upstairs loft.

Nightclubs

Banff has two nightclubs. Cavernous **Aurora** (downstairs in the Clock Tower Mall at 110 Banff Ave., 403/760-5300) was formerly an infamous gathering place known as Silver City, but renovations in the late 1990s added some class to Banff's clubbing scene. It's respectable early in the evening but becomes one obnoxiously loud, overpriced smoky pickup joint after midnight. The other option is **Hoo Doos** (at 137 Banff Ave., but enter from Caribou St., 403/762-8434), a stylish setup with similar citylike surroundings.

FESTIVALS AND EVENTS

Spring

Most of the major spring events take place at local winter resorts, including a variety of snowboard competitions that make for great spectator viewing. At Lake Louise a half pipe and jump are constructed right in front of the day lodge for this specific purpose. One long-running spring event is the **Slush Cup,** which takes place at Sunshine Village (www.skibanff.com) in late May. Events include kamikaze skiers and boarders who attempt to skim across an almost-frozen pit of water. While winter enthusiasts are at higher elevations, swooshing down the slopes of some of North America's latest-closing resorts, early May sees the Banff Springs Golf Course open for the season.

During the second week of June, the **Banff World Television Festival** (403/678-1216, www.banfftvfest.com) attracts 1,500 of the world's best television directors, producers, writers, and even actors for meetings, workshops, and awards, with many show screenings open to the public. For many delegates, pitching their ideas is what draws them to this event. The main venue is the Fairmont Banff Springs.

Summer

Summer is a time of hiking and camping, so festivals are few and far between. The main event is the **Banff Summer Arts Festival** (403/762-6301 or 800/413-8368, www.banffcentre.ca), a three-week (mid-July–early Aug.) extravaganza presented by professional artists studying at the Banff Centre. They perform dance, drama, opera, and jazz for the public at locations around town. Look for details in the *Crag and Canyon.*

On July 1, Banff kicks off **Canada Day** with a pancake breakfast on the grounds of the Park Administration Building. Then there's a full day of fun and frivolity in both Central and Banff Avenue Parks that includes events such as a stupid pet tricks competition. An impressive parade begins at 5 P.M., followed by a concert in Central Park and fireworks.

Each summer the national park staff presents an extensive **Park Interpretive Program** at locations in town and throughout the park, including downstairs in the visitors center at 8:30 P.M. daily. All programs are free and include guided hikes, nature tours, slide shows, campfire talks, and lectures. For details, consult *The Mountain Guide,* available at the Banff Visitor Centre (403/762-1550), or look for postings on campground bulletin boards.

Fall

Fall is the park's quietest season, but it's busiest in terms of festivals and events. First of the fall events, on the last Saturday in September, **Melissa's Road Race** (www.melissasroadrace.ca) attracts more than 2,000 runners (the race sells out months in advance) in 10- and 22-kilometer (6- and 14-mile) races. The **International Banff Springs Wine and Food Festival** (www.fairmont.com/banffsprings) is hosted by the Fairmont Banff Springs at the end of October. To encourage tourism during the quietest time of the year, **Winterstart** (Nov.–mid-Dec.) features cheap lodging and a host of fun events. This coincides with the opening of lifts at the park's three winter resorts beginning in mid-November.

One of the year's biggest events is the **Banff Mountain Film Festival,** held on the first weekend of November. Mountain-adventure

© ANDREW HEMPSTEAD

Canada Day in Central Park

filmmakers from around the world submit films to be judged by a select committee. Films are then shown throughout the weekend to an enthusiastic crowd of thousands. Exhibits and seminars are also presented, and top climbers and mountaineers from around the world are invited as guest speakers.

Tickets to the Banff Mountain Film Festival go on sale one year in advance and sell out quickly. Tickets for daytime shows start at $45 (for up to 10 films). Night shows are from $38, and all-weekend passes cost around $180 (weekend passes with two nights' accommodations and breakfasts start at a reasonable $290). Films are shown in the two theaters of the Banff Centre. For more information, contact the festival office (403/762-6675); for tickets, contact the Banff Centre box office (403/762-6301 or 800/413-8368, www.banffcentre.ca). If you miss the actual festival, it hits the road on the Best of the Festival World Tour. Look for it in your town, or check out www.banffcentre.ca for venues and dates.

Starting in the days leading up to the film festival, then running in conjunction with it,

is the **Banff Mountain Book Festival,** which showcases publishers, writers, and photographers whose work revolves around the world's great mountain ranges. Tickets can be bought to individual events ($16–30), or there's a Book Festival Pass ($130) and a pass combining both festivals ($280).

Winter

By mid-December lifts at all local winter resorts are open. **Santa Claus** makes an appearance on Banff Avenue at noon on the last Saturday in November; if you miss him there, he usually goes skiing at each of the local resorts on Christmas Day. Events at the resorts continue throughout the long winter season, among them **World Cup Downhill** skiing at Lake Louise in late November. The **Banff/Lake Louise Winter Festival** is a 10-day celebration at the end of January that has been a part of Banff's history since 1917. Look for ice sculpting on the frozen lake in front of the Chateau Lake Louise, the Lake Louise Loppet, barn dancing, and the Town Party, which takes place in the Fairmont Banff Springs.

SHOPPING

It may seem a little strange, but city folk from Calgary actually drive into Banff National Park to shop for clothes. This reflects the number of clothing shops in Banff rather than a lack of choice in one of Canada's largest cities.

Canadiana and Clothing

Few companies in the world were as responsible for the development of a country as was the **Hudson's Bay Company** (HBC) in Canada. Founded in 1670, the HBC established trading posts throughout western Canada, many of which attracted settlers, forming the nucleus for towns and cities that survive today, including Alberta's capital, Edmonton. HBC stores continue their traditional role of providing a wide range of goods, in towns big and small across the country. In Banff, the HBC store is at 125 Banff Avenue (403/762-5525).

Another Canadian store, this one famous for its fleeces, sweaters, leather goods, and as supplier to the Canadian Olympic teams, is **Roots** (227 Banff Ave., 403/762-9434). For belts, buckles, and boots, check out the **Trail Rider Store** (132 Banff Ave., 403/762-4551). Check out the **Rude Boys Snowboard Shop** (215 Banff Ave., 403/762-8480), downstairs in the Sundance Mall, but don't expect to find anything suitable for your grandparents.

Camping and Outdoor Gear

Inexpensive camping equipment and supplies can be found in **Home Hardware** (221 Bear St., 403/762-2080) and in the low-ceilinged downstairs section of the **Hudson's Bay Company** (125 Banff Ave., 403/762-5525). More specialized needs are catered to at **Mountain Magic Equipment** (224 Bear St., 403/762-2591). The store stocks a large range of top-quality outdoor and survival gear (including climbing equipment) and rents tents ($20 per day), sleeping bags ($12), backpacks ($10), and boots ($10). Mountain Magic Equipment also sells and repairs all types of bikes.

Two of the best spots to shop for outdoor apparel are locally owned **Abominable Ski & Sportswear** (229 Banff Ave., 403/762-2905) and **Monod Sports** (129 Banff Ave., 403/762-4571).

Gifts and Galleries

Banff's numerous galleries display the work of mostly Canadian artists. **Canada House Gallery** (201 Bear St., 403/762-3757) features a wide selection of Canadian landscape and wildlife works and native art. The **Quest Gallery** (105 Banff Ave., 403/762-2722) offers a diverse range of affordable Canadian paintings and crafts, as well as more exotic pieces such as mammoth tusks from prehistoric times and Inuit carvings from Nunavut. Browse through traditional native arts and crafts at the **Indian Trading Post** (1 Birch Ave., 403/762-2456), across the Bow River from downtown.

ACCOMMODATIONS AND CAMPING

Finding a room in Banff National Park in summer is nearly as hard as trying to justify its price. By late afternoon just about every room and campsite in the park will be occupied, and basic hotel rooms start at $100. Fortunately, many alternatives are available. Rooms in private homes begin at around $50 s, $60 d. HI–Banff Alpine Centre has dormitory-style accommodations for $29 per person per night. Bungalows or cabins can be rented, which can be cost-effective for families or small groups. Approximately 2,400 campsites in 13 campgrounds accommodate campers. Wherever you decide to stay, it is vital to book well ahead during summer and the Christmas holidays. The park's off-season is October–May, and hotels offer huge rate reductions during this period. Shop around, and you'll find many bargains.

All rates quoted are for a standard room in the high season (June–September).

In and Around the Town of Banff

Banff has a few accommodations right downtown, but most are strung out along Banff Avenue, an easy walk from the shopping and dining precinct. Nearby Tunnel Mountain is also home to a cluster of accommodations.

UNDER $50

The only beds in town less than $50 are in dormitories, and therefore, although rates are well less than $50, this is a per-person rate.

HI-Banff Alpine Centre (801 Hidden Ridge Way, 403/762-4123 or 866/762-4122, www.hihostels.ca) is just off Tunnel Mountain Road, three kilometers (1.9 miles) from downtown. This large, modern hostel sleeps 216 in small two-, four-, and six-bed dormitory rooms as well as four-bed cabins. The large lounge area has a fireplace, and other facilities include a recreation room, public Internet access, bike and ski/snowboard workshop, large kitchen, self-service café/bar, and laundry. In summer, members of Hostelling International pay $33 per person per night (nonmembers $37) for a dorm bed or $83 s or d ($88 for nonmembers) in a private room. The rest of the year, dorm beds are $27 (nonmembers $31) and private rooms $84 s or d (nonmembers $92). During July and August, reserve at least one month in advance to be assured of a bed. The hostel is open all day, but check-in isn't until midday. To get there from town, ride the Banff Transit bus ($2), which passes the hostel twice an hour during summer. The rest of the year the only transportation is by cab, about $7 from the bus depot.

A one-time hospital, **Banff Y Mountain Lodge** (102 Spray Ave., 403/762-3560 or 800/813-4138, www.ymountainlodge.com, dorm $33, $88 s, $99 d) has undergone massive renovations to create an excellent, centrally located choice for budget travelers. Facilities include the casual Sundance Bistro (7 A.M.–10 P.M.), a laundry facility, wireless Internet, and the Great Room—a huge living area where the centerpiece is a massive stone fireplace, with writing desks and shelves stocked with books scattered throughout. Some private rooms have en suites, while family rooms are $135. Rates are reduced outside of summer.

Along the main strip of accommodations and a five-minute walk to downtown is **Samesun Banff Chalet** (433 Banff Ave., 403/762-4499 or 877/972-6378, www.samesun.com, dorm $35, private $149 s or d). As converted motel rooms, each small dormitory has its own bathroom. Guest amenities include a lounge, wireless Internet, free continental breakfast, and underground parking. Slightly farther from downtown, **Samesun Banff Hostel** (449 Banff Ave., 403/762-5521, www.samesun.com, dorm $33, private from $89 s or d) has older rooms but is set around a pleasant courtyard.

$50-100

Accommodations in this price range are limited to private rooms at HI–Banff Alpine Centre, Banff Y Mountain Lodge, and Samesun Banff Chalet, and at a few bed-and-breakfasts. The best value of these is **Mountain View B&B** (347 Grizzly St., 403/760-9353, www.mountainviewbanff.ca, May–Sept., $95–130 s or d), on a quiet residential street three blocks from the heart of downtown. The two guest rooms are simply furnished, each with a double bed, TV, sink, and bar fridge. They share a bathroom and a common area that includes basic cooking facilities (microwave, toaster, kettle) and opens to a private deck. Off-street parking and a light breakfast round out this excellent choice.

$100-150

◖ Blue Mountain Lodge (137 Muskrat St., 403/762-5134, www.bluemtnlodge.com, $105–109 s, $129–179 d) is a rambling, older-style lodge with 10 guest rooms, each with a private bath, TV, and telephone. The Trapper's Cabin room is the most expensive, but the gabled ceiling, walls decorated with snowshoes and bearskin, and an electric fireplace create a funky, mountain feel. All guests have use of shared kitchen facilities, a lounge, and Internet access while enjoying an expansive cold buffet breakfast to set you up for a day of hiking.

Mountain Country Bed and Breakfast (427 Marten St., 403/762-3288, www.banffmountaincountry.com, $100–140 s or d) is a solid choice for traditional bed-and-breakfast accommodation. The longtime-local owners have created a home-away-from-home atmosphere in a single-family home along a residential street just a short walk from Banff Avenue.

The eight guest rooms at the **Elkhorn Lodge**

(124 Spray Ave., 403/762-2299 or 877/818-8488, www.elkhornbanff.ca, from $135) are nothing special, but travelers on a budget who aren't fans of bed-and-breakfasts will find this older lodge suitable. The four small sleeping rooms—each with a bathroom, TV, and coffeemaker—are $135 s or d, while larger rooms with fridges are $195–265. Rates include a light breakfast. It's halfway up the hill to the Fairmont Banff Springs.

Bumper's Inn is at the far end of the motel strip (603 Banff Ave., 403/762-3386 or 800/661-3518, www.bumpersinn.com, $125–145 s or d). The property is best known for its steakhouse, but behind the restaurant are 39 older-style rooms facing a courtyard for $145 s or d (from $85 in winter).

Two blocks off Banff Avenue, the **Homestead Inn** (217 Lynx St., 403/762-4471 or 800/661-1021, www.homesteadinnbanff.com, $129–139 s or d) is a lot closer to downtown than Bumper's. It's a fairly basic hostelry with a faux Tudor exterior, 27 guest rooms, and adjacent good-value restaurant.

$150-200

Some of Banff's private residences have cabins for rent. One of the reasons that **(Country Cabin Bed & Breakfast** (419 Beaver St., 403/762-3591, www.banffmountaincountry.com/cabin, $150 s or d) is the best of these is the quiet location off busy Banff Avenue that is still within easy walking distance of downtown. The log cabin has a separate bedroom, a full bathroom with log and tile features surrounding a jetted tub, and a living area equipped with a fold-out futon and a TV/VCR combo. If you don't feel like dining downtown, you can cook up a storm on the barbecue supplied. Rates are reduced to $85 outside of summer.

The rooms at the **Banff Inn** (501 Banff Ave., 403/762-8844, www.banffinn.com, $179–279 s or d) are no-frills modern in appearance. Each of the 99 rooms has a small log-trimmed balcony, and the facade is Rundlestone (quarried locally and named for Mount Rundle). Pluses include underground heated parking, a day spa, a guest lounge with fireplace and plasma TV, and free continental breakfast.

The days of Banff motel rooms for less than $100 disappeared in 2001 when bulldozers took to the town's last remaining park-at-your-door motel, the **Spruce Grove Inn** (545 Banff Ave., 403/762-3301 or 800/879-1991, www.banffsprucegroveinn.com, $165–275 s or d), now replaced by a modern mountain-style lodge of the same name. Rooms are spacious and a relatively good value at $185 s or d (upgrade to a king bed for $200 s or d or a Loft Suite that sleeps four for $225).

Toward downtown from the Spruce Grove is the **High Country Inn** (419 Banff Ave., 403/762-2236 or 800/293-5142, www.banffhighcountryinn.com, from $175 s or d), which has a heated indoor pool, spacious hot tubs, a cedar-lined sauna, and the ever-popular Ticino Swiss/Italian restaurant. All rooms are adequately furnished with comfortable beds and an earthy color scheme. The High Country's Honeymoon Suite ($285) is an excellent value; it features a king-size bed, fireplace, jetted tub, and a large balcony with views to Cascade Mountain.

The **Rundlestone Lodge** (537 Banff Ave., 403/762-2201 or 800/661-8630, www.rundlestone.com, $195–230 s or d) features mountain-style architecture with an abundance of raw stonework and exposed timber inside and out. At street level is a comfortable sitting area centered on a fireplace, as well as an indoor pool, a lounge-style bar, and a restaurant. Furniture and fittings in the 96 rooms are elegant, and all come with high-speed Internet access and a TV/DVD combo. Many rooms have small balconies and gas fireplaces; some are wheelchair accessible.

$200-250

More than 100 years since Jim and Bill Brewster guided their first guests through the park, their descendants are still actively involved in the tourist industry, operating the central and very stylish **(Brewster's Mountain Lodge** (208 Caribou St., 403/762-2900 or 888/762-2900, www.brewstermountainlodge.com). The building features an eye-catching log exterior with an equally impressive lobby. The Western theme is continued in the 77 upstairs rooms. Standard rooms feature two queen-size beds ($220), deluxe rooms offer a jetted tub and sitting area ($240), and loft suites are designed for families (from $280). Packages provide good value here, while off-season rates are slashed up to 50 percent.

The 134-room **Banff Ptarmigan Inn** (337 Banff Ave., 403/762-2207 or 800/661-8310, www.bestofbanff.com, $245 s or d) is a slick, full-service hotel with tastefully decorated rooms, down comforters on all beds, the Meatball Italian restaurant, heated underground parking, wireless Internet, and a variety of facilities to soothe sore muscles, including a spa, a whirlpool, and a sauna.

At the downtown end of the motel strip, guests at the **Banff International Hotel** (333 Banff Ave., 403/762-5666 or 800/665-5666, www.banffinternational.com, from $255) enjoy an abundance of in-room facilities, oak furniture, and marble bathrooms. Standard rooms are $255 s or d; the much larger corner rooms have mountain views and cost $325.

The following two accommodations are on Tunnel Mountain Road, a 15-minute downhill walk to town. Although falling in the same price range as many of those on Banff Avenue, all units are self-contained, making them good for families, small groups, or those who want to cook their own meals.

Opened as a bungalow camp in 1946, **Douglas Fir Resort** (403/762-5591 or 800/661-9267, www.douglasfir.com, $240 s or d) is now a sprawling complex of 133 large condo-style units. Each has a fully equipped kitchen and a lounge with fireplace. Other facilities include a hot tub, an exercise room, squash and tennis courts, a grocery store, and a laundry. Infinitely more important if you have children are the two indoor waterslides and heated pool. Check online for packages year-round.

Hidden Ridge Resort (403/762-3544 or 800/661-1372, www.bestofbanff.com, $220–540 s or d) sits on a forested hillside away from the main buzz of traffic. Choose from modern condo-style units to much larger Premier King Jacuzzi Suites. All units have wood-burning fireplaces, wireless Internet, and balconies or patios, and the condos have washer/dryer combos. In the center of the complex is a barbecue area and 30-person hot tub.

$250-300

In the heart of downtown Banff, the venerable **Mount Royal Hotel** (138 Banff Ave., 403/762-3331 or 877/442-2623, www.mountroyalhotel.com, $259 s or d) first opened in 1908. Since its purchase by the Brewster Transport Company in 1912, this distinctive redbrick building has seen various expansions and a disastrous fire in 1967, which destroyed the original wing. Today guests are offered 135 tastefully decorated rooms with high-speed Internet access and the use of a large health club with hot tub. Also on the premises are a restaurant and small lounge. For a splurge, you won't find better than the one-bedroom suites ($299–429).

Best rooms along the motel strip are at **Delta Banff Royal Canadian Lodge** (459 Banff Ave., 403/762-3307 or 888/778-5050, www.deltahotels.com, from $290 s or d), which opened in the summer of 2000. It features 99 luxuriously appointed rooms, heated underground parking, a lounge, a dining room where upscale Canadian specialties are the highlight, a large spa/pool complex, and a landscaped courtyard.

OVER $300

At **Buffalo Mountain Lodge,** a 15-minute walk from town on Tunnel Mountain Road (Tunnel Mountain Dr., 403/762-2400 or 800/661-1367, www.crmr.com, $319 s or d), you'll notice the impressive timber-frame construction, as well as the hand-hewn construction of the lobby, with its vaulted ceiling and eye-catching fieldstone fireplace. The 108 rooms, chalets, and bungalows all have fireplaces, balconies, large bathrooms, and comfortable beds topped by feather-filled duvets; many have kitchens. And you won't need to go to town to eat—one of Banff's best restaurants, Cilantro Mountain

Café, is adjacent to the main lodge. Although rack rates start over $300, book in advance and online to pick up summer rates around $250. (The lodge takes its name from Tunnel Mountain, which early park visitors called Buffalo Mountain, for its shape.)

Bed-and-breakfast connoisseurs will fall in love with **Buffaloberry B&B** (417 Marten St., 403/762-3750, www.buffaloberry.com, $325 s or d), a purpose-built lodging within walking distance of downtown. The home itself is a beautiful timber and stone structure, while inside, guests soak up mountain-style luxury in the vaulted living area, which comes complete with a stone fireplace, super comfortable couches, and a library of local books. The spacious rooms come with niceties such as pillow-top mattresses, TV/DVD combos, heated bathroom floors, and bathrobes. Buffaloberry is also the only local bed-and-breakfast with heated underground parking.

The 770-room **Fairmont Banff Springs** (403/762-2211 or 800/257-7544, www.fairmont.com, $439 s or d) is Banff's best-known accommodation. Earlier this century, the hotel came under the ownership of Fairmont Hotels and Resorts, losing its century-old tag as a Canadian Pacific hotel and in the process its ties to the historic railway company that constructed the original hotel back in 1888. Even though the rooms have been modernized, many date to the 1920s, and as is common in older establishments, these accommodations are small (Fairmont Rooms are 14.4 square meters/155 square feet). But room size is only a minor consideration when staying in this historic gem. With 12 eateries, four lounges, a luxurious spa facility, a huge indoor pool, elegant public spaces, a 27-hole golf course, tennis courts, horseback riding, and enough twisting, turning hallways, towers, and shops to warrant a detailed map, you'll not be wanting to spend much time in your room. Unless, of course, you are in the eight-room presidential suite. During summer, rack rates for a regular Fairmont room are $439 (s or d), discounted to around $350 the rest of the year. Many summer visitors stay as part of a package—the place to find these is on the website www.fairmont.com.

Packages may simply include breakfast, while others will have you golfing, horseback riding, or relaxing in the spa.

On Mountain Avenue, a short walk from the Upper Hot Springs, is **Rimrock Resort Hotel** (403/762-3356 or 888/746-7625, www.rimrockresort.com, $355–455 s or d). The original hotel was constructed in 1903 but was fully rebuilt and opened as a full-service luxury resort in the mid-1990s. Guest amenities include two restaurants, two lounges, a health club, an outdoor patio, and a multistory parking garage. Each of 345 well-appointed rooms is decorated with earthy tones offset by brightly colored fabrics. They also feature picture windows, a king-size bed, a comfortable armchair, a writing desk, two phones, a minibar, and a hair dryer. Since it's set high above the Bow Valley, views for the most part are excellent.

Along the Bow Valley Parkway and Vicinity

The Bow Valley Parkway is the original route between Banff and Lake Louise. It is a beautiful drive in all seasons, and along its length are several accommodations, each a viable alternative to staying in Banff.

UNDER $50

Thirty-two kilometers (20 miles) from Banff along the Bow Valley Parkway, **HI-Castle Mountain** is near several interesting hikes and across the road from a general store with basic supplies. This hostel sleeps 28 in two dorms and has a kitchen, octagonal common room with wood-burning fireplace, hot showers, and bike rentals. Members of Hostelling International pay $23, nonmembers $27. Make bookings through the association's reservation line (866/762-4122) or book online (www.hihostels.ca). Check-in is 5–10 P.M.

$100-150

Johnston Canyon Resort (403/762-2971 or 888/378-1720, www.johnstoncanyon.com, mid-May–early Oct., $149–314 s or d) is 26 kilometers (16 miles) west of Banff at the beginning of a short trail that leads to the famous canyon. The rustic cabins are older, and some have kitchenettes. On the grounds are tennis courts, a barbecue area, and a general store. Resort dining options are as varied as munching on a burger and fries at the counter of an old-time cafeteria to enjoying pan-fried rainbow trout in a dining room that oozes alpine charm. Basic two-person duplex cabins are $149, two-person cabins with a gas fireplace and sitting area are $189, and they go up in price all the way to $314 for a classic bungalow complete with two bedrooms, cooking facilities, and heritage-style furnishings.

$150-200

Constructed by the Canadian Pacific Railway in 1922, **C Storm Mountain Lodge** (Hwy. 93, 403/762-4155, www.stormmountainlodge.com, early Dec.–mid-Oct., $169–289) reopened in 2003 after a major restoration project that saw 14 historic cabins returned to their former rustic glory. Each has its original log walls, along with a log bed, covered deck, a wood-burning fireplace, and bathroom with claw-foot tub. They don't have phones or TVs, so there's little to distract you from the past. Off-season deals include a breakfast and dinner package (mid-April–mid-June) for $225 d. Outside, the wilderness beckons, with Storm Mountain as a backdrop. The lodge is at Vermilion Pass, a 25-minute drive from Banff or Lake Louise (head west from the Castle Mountain interchange). The lodge restaurant (daily 7:30–10:30 A.M. and 5–9 P.M.) is one of my favorite places to eat in the park.

OVER $200

C Baker Creek Chalets (403/522-3761, www.bakercreek.com, $290–365 s or d) lies along the Bow Valley Parkway 40 kilometers (25 miles) northwest of Banff and 10 kilometers (6.2 miles) from Lake Louise. Each of the log chalets has a kitchenette, loft, fireplace, and outside deck (complete with cute wood carvings of bears climbing over the railings). The Trapper's Cabin is a huge space with a log bed, antler chandelier, wood-burning fireplace, double-jetted tub, and cooking facilities.

Baker Creek Chalets

A lodge wing has eight luxurious suites, each with richly accented log work, a deck, a microwave and fridge, and a deluxe bathroom. (Check the website for great off-season deals.) The restaurant here is highly recommended.

At Castle Junction, 32 kilometers (20 miles) northwest of Banff, is **Castle Mountain Chalets** (403/762-3868 or 877/762-2281, www.castlemountain.com, $255-335 s or d). Set on 1.5 hectares (four acres), this resort is home to a collection of magnificent log chalets. Each has high ceilings, beautifully handcrafted log interiors, at least two beds, a stone fireplace, a full kitchen with dishwasher, a bathroom with hot tub, and satellite TV. At the back of the grounds are several older cabins offered in summer ($190 s or d). Part of the complex is a grocery store, barbecue area, and the only gas between Banff and Lake Louise. The nearest restaurants are at Baker Creek Chalets and Johnston Canyon Resort.

BACKCOUNTRY ACCOMMODATIONS
Brewster's Shadow Lake Lodge (403/762-0116

or 866/762-0114, www.shadowlakelodge.com, mid-June–Sept.) is 14 kilometers (8.7 miles) from the nearest road. Access is on foot or, in winter, on skis. The lodge is near picturesque Shadow Lake, and many hiking trails are nearby. Dating to 1928, the oldest structure has been restored as a rustic yet welcoming dining area, with a woodstove in the kitchen. Guests overnight in 12 newer, comfortable cabins, while in a separate building you find washrooms with showers. The daily rate, including three meals served buffet-style and afternoon tea, is $192 per person per day. The trailhead is along the TransCanada Highway, 19 kilometers (12 miles) from Banff, at the Redearth Creek parking area. In February and March, when access is on cross-country skis, the lodge is open Thursday–Sunday and rates are $140 per person.

Campgrounds

Within Banff National Park, 13 campgrounds hold more than 2,000 sites. Although the town of Banff has five of these facilities with more than 1,500 sites in its immediate vicinity, most fill by early afternoon. The three largest campgrounds are strung out over 1.5 kilometers (0.9 mile) along Tunnel Mountain Road, with the nearest sites 2.5 kilometers (1.6 miles) from town. A percentage of sites at Tunnel Mountain Campground can be reserved through the **Parks Canada Campground Reservation Service** (877/737-3783, www.pccamping. ca), and it's strongly recommended that you do reserve if you require electrical hookups. Although plenty of sites are available for those without reservations, they fill fast each day (especially in July and August). The official checkout time is 11 A.M., so plan on arriving at your campground of choice earlier in the day than this to ensure getting a site. At more popular locations on summer weekends, a line forms, waiting for sites to become vacant. This is especially true at the Banff and Lake Louise campgrounds, which offer powered sites. When the main campgrounds fill, those unable to secure a site will be directed to an overflow area along Minnewanka Lake Road. These provide few

facilities and no hookups but cost less. Open fires are permitted in designated areas throughout all campgrounds, but you must purchase a Firewood Permit ($6 per site per night) to burn wood, which is provided at no cost. For general camping information, stop at the Banff Visitor Centre (224 Banff Ave., 403/762-1550) or go the Parks Canada website, www.pc.gc.ca, and follow the links to Banff National Park.

AROUND THE TOWN OF BANFF

Closest to town is **Tunnel Mountain Campground,** which is three campgrounds rolled into one. The location is a lightly treed ridge east of downtown, with views north to Cascade Mountain and south to Mount Rundle. From town, follow Tunnel Mountain Road east, to beyond the Douglas Fir Resort (which is within walking distance for groceries, liquor, and laundry). If you're coming in off the TransCanada Highway from the east, bypass town completely by turning left onto Tunnel Mountain Road at the Banff Rocky Mountain Resort. Approaching from this direction, the first campground you pass is the park's largest, with 622 well-spaced, relatively private sites ($28 per site), each with a fire ring and picnic table. Other amenities include drinking water, hot showers, and kitchen shelters. This campground has no hookups. It is open mid-May–early September. Less than one kilometer (0.6 mile) farther along Tunnel Mountain Road toward town is a signed turnoff (Hookups) that leads to a registration booth for two more campgrounds. Unless you have a reservation from Parks Canada Campground Reservation Service (877/737-3783, www.pccamping.ca), you'll be asked whether you require an electrical hookup ($32 per site) or a site with power, water, and sewer ($38 per site), then sent off into the corresponding campground. The power-only section (closest to town) stays open year-round, the other mid-May–September. Both have hot showers but little privacy between sites.

Along Lake Minnewanka Road northeast of town are two campgrounds offering fewer services than the others, but with sites that offer more privacy. The pick of the two is **Two Jack**

© ANDREW HEMPSTEAD

RV camping in Banff National Park

Lakeside Campground (June–mid-Sept., $32 per site), with 80 sites tucked into trees at the south end of Two Jack Lake, an extension of Lake Minnewanka. Facilities include hot showers, kitchen shelters, drinking water, and flush toilets. It's just over six kilometers (3.7 miles) from the TransCanada Highway underpass. The much larger **Two Jack Main Campground** (mid-June–mid-Sept., $22 per site) is a short distance farther along the road, with 381 sites spread throughout a shallow valley. It offers the same facilities as Two Jack Lakeside, sans showers. The overflow camping area ($10) for these and the three Tunnel Mountain campgrounds is at the beginning of the Lake Minnewanka Road loop.

BOW VALLEY PARKWAY

Along Bow Valley Parkway between the town of Banff and Lake Louise are three campgrounds. Closest to Banff is **Johnston Canyon Campground** (early June–mid-Sept., $28 per site), between the road and the rail line, 26 kilometers (16 miles) west of Banff. It is the largest of the three campgrounds, with 140 sites, and has hot showers but no hookups. Almost directly opposite is Johnston Canyon Resort, with groceries and a restaurant, and the beginning of a trail to the park's best-known waterfalls.

Continuing eight kilometers (five miles) toward Lake Louise, **Castle Mountain Campground** (early June–early Sept., $22 per site) is also within walking distance of a grocery store (no restaurant), but it has just 44 sites and no showers. Services are limited to flush toilets, drinking water, and kitchen shelters.

Protection Mountain Campground (July–Aug., $22 per site), a further 14 kilometers (8.7 miles) west and just over 20 kilometers (12.5 miles) from Lake Louise, opens as demand dictates, usually by late June. It offers 89 sites, along with flush toilets, drinking water, and stove-equipped kitchen shelters.

FOOD

Whether you're in search of an inexpensive snack for the family or silver service, you can find it in the town of Banff, which has over 100 restaurants (more per capita than any town or city across Canada). The quality of food varies greatly. Some restaurants revolve solely around the tourist trade, while others have reputations that attract diners from Calgary who have been known to stay overnight just to eat at their favorite haunt. While the quality of food is most people's number one priority when dining out, the level of service (or lack of it) also comes into play in Banff, especially if you are paying big bucks for a fine-dining meal. Getting it all right—good food, top-notch service, and a memorable ambience—in a tourism-oriented town is rare. Which leads to the restaurants I've recommended below, the best of a very varied bunch.

Groceries

Banff has two major grocery stores. In addition to a wide selection of basic groceries, **Nesters Market** (122 Bear St., 403/762-3663, 8 A.M.–11 P.M. daily in summer, shorter hours the rest of the year) has a good deli with premade salads and sandwiches, soups to go, and hot chicken. At the other end of downtown is **Safeway** (318 Marten St., 403/762-5329, 8 A.M.–11 P.M. daily).

Cafés and Coffee Shops

Banff's lone bakery is [**Wild Flour** (Bison Courtyard, 211 Bear St., 403/760-5074, 7 A.M.–6 P.M. daily, $5–10), and it's a good one (albeit a little pricey). Organic ingredients are used whenever possible, and everything is freshly baked daily. The result is an array of healthy breads, mouthwatering cakes and pastries, and delicious meat pies. Eat inside or out.

Evelyn's Coffee Bar (119 and 201 Banff Ave., 403/762-0352, sandwiches $7) has two central locations pouring good coffee and serving huge sandwiches. The few outside tables at 201 Banff Avenue—on the busiest stretch of the busiest street in town—are perfect for people-watching. The **Cake Company** (220 Bear St., 403/762-8642, cakes $4) is another local place serving great coffee and delicious

enjoying a sunny morning in front of the Wild Flour bakery

© ANDREW HEMPSTEAD

pastries, muffins, and cakes baked daily on the premises. **Jump Start** (206 Buffalo St., 403/762-0332, $5.50–7), opposite Central Park, has a wide range of coffee concoctions as well as homemade soups and sandwiches.

Cheap Eats

A good place to begin looking for cheap eats is the Food Court in the lower level of Cascade Plaza (317 Banff Ave.). Here you'll find a juice bar, a place selling pizza by the slice, and **Banff Edo,** which sells simple Japanese dishes for around $7.50, including a drink. Also downtown is **Barpa Bill's** (223 Bear St., 403/762-0377, 11 A.M.–midnight daily, $8–12), a hole-in-the-wall eatery with a couple of indoor tables and a menu of inexpensive Greek dishes.

At the back of the Clock Tower Mall, **Pad Thai** (110 Banff Ave., 403/762-4911, lunch and dinner daily, $9–15) is a real find. The namesake pad Thai is $9, curries are all around the same price, and delicious spring rolls are $4. You can eat in or take out.

The main reasons for visiting the Banff

Evelyn's Coffee Bar is one of Banff's favorite cafés.

Centre include attending the many events, exercising at the fitness facility, or wandering through the grounds. Add to this list having a casual meal at the **Gooseberry Juice Bar** (Banff Centre, Tunnel Mountain Dr., 403/762-6100, 8 A.M.–10 P.M. daily, $5–8), overlooking the swimming pool within the Sally Borden Building. Sandwiches are made to order, or try a minipizza or bowl of steaming soup.

Cougar Pete's Cafe in the Banff Alpine Centre (off Tunnel Mountain Rd., 403/762-4122, breakfast, lunch, and dinner daily, $9–15) offers free wireless Internet and a great outdoor patio. The menu features all the usual café-style dishes, such as a pile of nachos for $9; no entrée is more than $15.

Aardvarks (304 Caribou St., 403/762-5500, noon–4 A.M. daily) is a late-night pizza hangout.

Family-Style Dining

In the Banff Caribou Lodge is **The Keg** (521 Banff Ave., 403/762-4442, 7 A.M.–2 A.M. daily, $16–28), part of a restaurant chain that began in Vancouver, which is noted for its consistently good steak, seafood, and chicken dishes at reasonable prices. It's also known for upbeat, well-presented servers. All entrées include a 60-item salad bar. Another Keg is downtown (117 Banff Ave., 403/760-3030).

Earls (299 Banff Ave., 403/762-4414, lunch and dinner daily, $18–32) has more of the same at slightly higher prices. This Alberta-born chain has a reputation for a menu of fusion cuisine that follows food trends, employs bright young servers, and offers a fun atmosphere.

Children will love the food and parents will love the prices at **Old Spaghetti Factory** (upstairs in the Cascade Plaza on Banff Ave., 403/760-2779, from 11:30 A.M. daily, $9.50–20). The room is casual-rustic, with a few tables spread along a balcony. Sort through a maze of combinations and specials (kids get their own color-in menu), and the most you'll pay for a meal is $20, which includes soup or salad, a side of bread, dessert, and coffee.

Steak

Alberta beef is mostly raised on ranchland east

of the park and features prominently on menus throughout town. Finely marbled AAA beef is used in most restaurants and is unequaled in its tender, juicy qualities.

Even though **Bumper's** (603 Banff Ave., 403/762-2622, 4:30–10 P.M. daily, $18–34) is away from the center of Banff, it's worth leaving the shopping strip and heading out to this popular steakhouse. Large cuts of Alberta beef, an informal atmosphere, efficient service, and great prices keep people coming back. Favorite choices are the slabs of roast prime rib of beef, in four sizes of cuts and cooked to order. Prices range from $18 for the Ladies cut to $34 for the Man Mountain cut, which includes unlimited trips to a small salad bar. Upstairs is the **Loft Lounge,** a good place to wait for a table or relax afterward with an inexpensive drink.

Considered one of Banff's most fashionable restaurants, **◖ Saltlik** (221 Bear St., 403/762-2467, from 11 A.M. daily, $21–39) is big and bold, and the perfect choice for serious carnivores with cash to spare. The concrete-and-steel split-level interior is complemented by modish wood furnishings. Facing the street, glass doors fold back to a terrace for warm-weather dining. The specialty is AAA Alberta beef, finished with grain feeding to enhance the flavor, then flash-seared at 650°C (1,200°F) to seal in the juices, and served with a side platter of seasonal vegetables. Entrées are priced comparable to a city steakhouse, but the cost creeps up as you add side dishes.

Casually Canadian

Of the many Banff drinking holes that offer pub-style menus, **Wild Bill's** (201 Banff Ave., 403/762-0333, 11 A.M.–after midnight daily, $10–21) is a standout. It's named for one of Banff's most famed mountain men, and the decor is suitably Western, with a menu to match. The nachos grande ($10.50) with a side of guacamole ($4) is perfect to share. Later in the day, flame-grilled T-bone steaks and spit-roasted chicken are traditional favorites ($15–30). Plan on dining before 9 P.M. to miss the crowd that arrives for the live music.

A town favorite that has faithfully served locals for many years is **Melissa's** (218 Lynx St., 403/762-5511, 7:30 A.M.–9:30 P.M. daily, $11–24), housed in a log building that dates from 1928 (the original Homestead Inn). Lunch and dinner are old-fashioned, casual affairs—choose from a wide variety of generously sized burgers, freshly prepared salads, and mouthwatering Alberta beef.

Bruno's Café & Grill (304 Caribou St., 403/762-8115, 7 A.M.–10 P.M. daily, $9–21), named for Bruno Engler, locally renowned photographer, ski instructor, and mountain man, is a cozy little café with a great mountain ambience and comfortable couches.

Classically Canadian

Buffalo Mountain Lodge Restaurant (Tunnel Mountain Rd., 403/762-2400, 7 A.M.–10 P.M. daily, $24–37), at the lodge of the same name, offers the perfect setting for a moderate splurge. It features a distinctive interior of hand-hewn cedar beams and old-world elegance—complete with stone fireplace and a chandelier made entirely from elk antlers—along with large windows that frame the surrounding forest. The featured cuisine is referred to as Rocky Mountain, reflecting an abundance of Canadian game and seafood combined with native berries and fruits. The least-expensive way to dine on this uniquely Canadian fare is by visiting at lunch and ordering the Rocky Mountain Game Platter, $20 for two people. Dinner entrées include fare like elk sirloin that's given an exotic touch with accompanying quince compote.

The food at **◖ Storm Mountain Lodge** (Hwy. 93, 403/762-4155, 7:30 A.M.–9 P.M. daily May–mid-Oct. and 5–9 P.M. Fri.–Sun. early Dec.–Apr., $24–36) is excellent, but it's the ambience you'll remember long after leaving—an intoxicating blend of historic appeal and rustic mountain charm. The chef uses mostly organic produce with seasonally available game and seafood—bison, venison, wild salmon, and the like—to create tasty and interesting dishes well suited to the I-must-be-in-the-Canadian-wilderness surroundings.

Storm Mountain Lodge is a 25-minute drive northwest from Banff; take the TransCanada Highway toward Lake Louise and head west at the Castle Mountain interchange.

Also well worth the drive is **⟨ The Bistro** (Baker Creek Chalets, 40 km/24.7 miles northwest of town along the Bow Valley Parkway, 403/522-2182, 7 A.M.–2 P.M. Sat.–Sun., noon–2 P.M. Mon.–Fri., and 5–9:30 P.M. daily, $18–34). Dining is in a small room that characterizes the term "mountain hideaway," in an adjacent lounge bar, or out on a small deck decorated with pots of colorful flowers. The menu isn't large, but dishes feature lots of Canadian game and produce, with favorites like beer-braised bison short ribs and cedar-planked salmon.

Canadian Contemporary

Occupying the prime position on one of Banff's busiest corners is the **Maple Leaf** (137 Banff Ave., 403/760-7680, 11 A.M.–11 P.M. daily, $21–37). Take in the dramatic Canadian-themed decor—exposed river stone, polished log work, a two-story interior rock wall, and a moose head (tucked around the corner from the street-level lounge). Some tables surround a busy area by the bar and kitchen, so try to talk your way into the upstairs back corner. The cooking uses modern styles with an abundance of Canadian game and produce. The lunch menu has a bison burger, along with lighter salads and gourmet sandwiches. Some of Canada's finest ingredients appear on the dinner menu: Stuffed halibut and the bacon-wrapped bison tenderloin are standouts. Treat yourself to a glass of Canadian ice wine to accompany dessert.

The Bison Restaurant and Lounge (Bison Courtyard, Bear St., 403/762-5550) is a two-story eatery featuring a casual lounge (daily for lunch and dinner, $10–28) downstairs and a more formal and expensive upstairs restaurant (daily for dinner, $26–45). The most sought-after tables at the downstairs lounge are outside in the courtyard, while inside is furniture ranging from painted tree stumps to a long bar. The chefs do an excellent job of sourcing top-notch local ingredients to create a delicious Caesar salad ($10), bison chili (also $10), and gourmet sandwiches ($13–17). Upstairs, in the main restaurant, the interesting decor sees chic-industrial blending with mountain rustic. Tables are inside or out at this upstairs dining

upstairs at The Bison Restaurant and Lounge

© ANDREW HEMPSTEAD

the deli counter at The Bison Restaurant and Lounge

room, and almost all have a view of the open kitchen. The food is solidly Canadian, with a menu that takes advantage of wild game, seafood, and Alberta beef. Also of note is the wine list, which again is extremely well priced, compared to other Banff restaurants.

《 Juniper Bistro (The Juniper, Norquay Rd., 403/763-6205, 7 A.M.–9:30 P.M. daily, $25–37) is well worth searching out for both Canadian cuisine and unparalleled views across town to Mount Rundle and the Spray Valley. The stylish interior may be inviting, but in warmer weather, you'll want to be outside on the patio, where the panorama is most spectacular. The menu blends traditional tastes with Canadian produce. If your taste runs toward seafood, there's grilled calamari ($11) as a starter. For those looking for something a little more local, the elk roast ($32) is a good choice. Most breakfasts are under $15, while at lunch, the Taste of the Rockies platter for two ($24) is a treat.

Banff's original bistro-style restaurant, which opened in the early 1990s, is **Coyote's** (206 Caribou St., 403/762-3963, 7:30 A.M.–10 P.M.

daily, $15–28). Meals are prepared in full view of diners, and the menu emphasizes fresh, health-conscious cooking, with just a hint of Southwestern style. To start, it's hard to go past the sweet potato and corn chowder ($6), and then choose from mains as varied as a simple Mediterranean-influenced pasta and a flank steak marinated in Cajun spices and topped with a generous dab of corn and tomato salsa.

European

Giorgio's (219 Banff Ave., 403/762-5114, daily for lunch and dinner, $16–29) has a casual old-world atmosphere. Its chefs prepare as many as 400 meals each afternoon, and the lineup for tables through summer is ever present. Classic pasta dishes start under $20, while fish and meat specialties top out at $29.

If you are staying up on Tunnel Mountain—or even if you're not—**《 Cilantro Mountain Café** (Buffalo Mountain Lodge, 403/760-3008, 11 A.M.–11 P.M. daily in summer, 5–10 P.M. Wed.–Sun. the rest of the year, closed mid-Sept.–mid-Dec., $15–28) is an excellent choice for a casual, well-priced meal. You can choose to dine inside the cozy log cabin that holds the main restaurant and open kitchen, or out on the patio. Starters are dominated by seafood options, but the flatbread, baked to order and delivered with choice of dips ($9), is a good choice to share. The thin-crust, wood-fired pizza for one is the highlight, with a small but varied selection of other mains that change as seasonal produce becomes available. Highly recommended if you want a break from Banff Avenue.

《 Ticino (High Country Inn, 415 Banff Ave., 403/762-3848, 5–10 P.M. daily, $15–38) reflects the heritage of the park's early mountain guides, with solid timber furnishings, lots of peeled and polished log work, and old wooden skis, huge cowbells, and an alpenhorn decorating the walls. It's named for the southern province of Switzerland, where the cuisine has a distinctive Italian influence. The Swiss chef is best known for a creamy wild mushroom soup, unique to the region; his beef and cheese fondues ($17–27 per person); juicy cuts of Alberta beef; and veal dishes (such as veal scaloppini; $27.50). Save room for one of Ticino's sinfully rich desserts. Also of note is professional service.

The **Balkan** (120 Banff Ave., 403/762-3454, 11 A.M.–11 P.M. daily, $11–24) is run by a local Greek family, but the menu blends their heritage with the cuisines of Italy, China, and Canada. Select from Greek ribs (pork ribs with a lemon sauce), the Greek chow mein (stir-fried vegetables, fried rice, and your choice of meat), or Greek spaghetti. But the most popular dishes are souvlaki and an enormous Greek platter for two.

You'll think you've swapped continents when you step into **Le Beaujolais** (212 Buffalo St., at Banff Ave., 403/762-2712, from 6 P.M. daily, $26–38), a Canadian leader in French cuisine. With crisp white linens, old-style stately decor, and immaculate service, this elegant room has been one of Banff's most popular fine-dining restaurants for 20 years. Its second-floor location ensures great views of Banff, especially from window tables. The dishes feature mainly Canadian produce, prepared and served with a traditional French flair. Entrées such as Alberta pork chop smothered in béarnaise sauce with a side of king crab meat range $26–38, but the extent of your final tab depends on whether you choose à la carte items or one of the three- and six-course table d'hôte menus ($74 and $98, respectively)—and also on how much wine you consume. Nationalism shows through in the 10,000-bottle cellar, with lots of reds from the Bordeaux and Burgundy regions of France. Reservations are necessary.

Fondue

Even if you've tried exotic meats, you probably haven't had them in a restaurant like the ◖ **Grizzly House** (207 Banff Ave., 403/762-4055, 11:30 A.M.–midnight daily, $18–32), which provides Banff's most unusual dining experience. The decor is, to say the least, eclectic (many say eccentric)—think lots of twisted woods, a motorbike hanging from the ceiling, a melted telephone on the wall. Each table has a phone for across-table conversation, or you can put a call through to your server, the

bar, a cab, diners in the private booth, or even those who spend too long in the bathroom. The food is equally unique, and the service is as professional as anywhere in town. The menu hasn't changed in decades, and this doesn't displease anyone. Most dining revolves around traditional Swiss fondues, but with nontraditional dipping meats such as rattlesnake, alligator, shark, ostrich, scallops, elk, and wild boar. Four-course table d'hôte fondue dinners are $44–62 per person, which includes soup or salad, followed by a cheese fondue, then a choice of one of six meat and seafood fondue (or hot rock) choices, and finally a fruity chocolate fondue. The Grizzly House is also open at lunch, when you can sample Canadian game at reduced prices; wild game meat loaf is $12, and an Alberta-farmed buffalo burger is $13.

Japanese

A couple of doors off Banff Avenue, **Sushi House Banff** (304 Caribou St., 403/762-2971, daily for lunch and dinner) is a tiny space with a dozen stools set around a moving miniature railway that has diners picking sushi and other delicacies from a train as it circles the chef,

Sushi House Banff

loading the carriages as quickly as they empty. Plates range $2.50–5.

More expensive is **Suginoya** (225 Banff Ave., 403/762-4773, 11 A.M.–10:30 P.M. daily, $14–24). Choose from the sushi bar, *ozashiki* booths, or regular tables. Traditional *shabu-shabu* and seafood teriyaki are staples. The number of Japanese diners here is indicative of the quality.

Fairmont Banff Springs

Whether guests or not, most visitors to Banff drop by to see one of the town's biggest tourist attractions, and a meal here might not be as expensive as you think. The hotel itself has more eateries than most small towns—from a deli serving slices of pizza to the finest of fine dining in the Banffshire Club.

If you are in the mood for a snack such as chili and bread or sandwiches to go, head to the lobby level and the **Castle Pantry,** which is open 24 hours daily.

Impressive buffets are the main draw at the **Bow Valley Grill,** a pleasantly laid out dining room that seats 275. Each morning from 6:30 A.M. an expansive buffet of hot and cold delicacies, including freshly baked bread and seasonal fruits, is laid out for the masses ($32 per person). Lunch (11:30 A.M.–5:30 P.M. daily) offers a wide-ranging menu featuring everything from salads to seafood. Through the busiest months of summer, a lunch buffet (11:30 A.M.–2 P.M. Mon.–Fri., 11:30 A.M.–4 P.M. Sat., $35) is offered. In summer, evening diners (6–9 P.M.) order from a menu that appeals to all tastes, while the rest of the year dinner is offered as a buffet, with a different theme each night. The Sunday brunch (11 A.M.–2:30 P.M., $45) is legendary, with chefs working at numerous stations scattered around the dining area and an enormous spread not equaled for variety anywhere in the mountains. Reservations are required for Sunday brunch (as far in advance as possible) and dinner.

Ensconced in an octagonal room of the Manor Wing, **Castello Ristorante** (6–9:30 P.M. Fri.–Tues., $18–32) is a seductive dining room with a modern, upscale ambience. The menu is dominated by Italian favorites, with traditional pastas and specialties such as veal tenderloin. The **Rundle Lounge & Hall** (from 11:30 A.M. daily) combines an area filled with comfortable sofas with summer outdoor dining and an upstairs piano bar, where most tables offer views down the Bow Valley. **Grapes** (6–9 P.M. daily, $14–26) is an intimate yet casual wine bar noted for its fine cheeses and pâtés. More substantial meals such as fondues are also offered.

The hotel's most acclaimed restaurant is the **Banffshire Club** (6–10 P.M. Tues.–Sat., $28–45), which seats just 65 diners. This fine-dining restaurant is a bastion of elegance, which begins as a harp player serenades you through a gated entrance. Inside, extravagantly rich wood furnishings, perfectly presented table settings, muted lighting, and kilted staff create an atmosphere as far removed from the surrounding wilderness as is imaginable. Reservations and a jacket are required.

Two restaurants lie within the grounds surrounding the hotel, and both are worthy of consideration. Originally the golf course clubhouse, the **Waldhaus Restaurant** (6–9 P.M. daily,

fondue at Waldhaus Restaurant

closed Apr., $21–29) is nestled in a forested area directly below the hotel. The big room is dominated by dark woods and is warmed by an open fireplace. The menu features German specialties, such as fondues. Below the restaurant is a pub of the same name, with a pub-style dinner menu offered in a casual atmosphere. The **Golf Course Clubhouse** (11:30 A.M.–5 P.M. daily in summer, $9–22) is a seasonal restaurant on the golf course proper that serves light breakfasts, lunch buffets, and more formal dinners. A shuttle bus runs every 30 minutes between the main lobby and the clubhouse.

For all Fairmont Banff Springs dining reservations, call 403/662-6860 or, after 5 P.M., 403/762-2211. During the summer months a desk in the main lobby has all menus posted and takes reservations.

INFORMATION

Many sources of information are available on the park and its commercial facilities. Once you've arrived, the best place to make your first stop is the **Banff Visitor Centre** (224

Banff Ave., 8 A.M.–8 P.M. daily mid-June–Aug., 8 A.M.–6 P.M. daily mid-May–mid-June and Sept., 9 A.M.–5 P.M. daily the rest of the year). This central complex houses information desks for **Parks Canada** (403/762-1550) and the **Banff/Lake Louise Tourism Bureau** (403/762-0270), as well as a Friends of Banff National Park shop, which stocks a good variety of park-related literature.

National Park Information

On the right-hand side of the **Banff Visitor Centre** is a row of desks staffed by Parks Canada employees. They will answer all of your queries regarding Banff's natural wonders and advise you of trail closures. Anyone planning an overnight backcountry trip should register here and obtain a camping pass ($10 per person per night). Also here, you can pick up park brochures, or wander down the back to peruse park maps, view a free slide show, and watch videos about the park. All questions pertaining to the national park itself can be answered here, or check out the Parks Canada website (www.pc.gc.ca).

© ANDREW HEMPSTEAD

Banff Visitor Centre

The park's **Warden's Office** (403/762-1470) is in the industrial park. The **weather office** (403/762-2088) offers updated forecasts. If you want to *see* the weather in Banff, check out the webcam at www.banffgondola.com. Tune in to FM 101.1 or go to www.friendsofbanff.com/parkradio.html to listen to Park Radio, which features daily updates and Banff-related programming.

Tourism Information

In the **Banff Visitor Centre,** across the floor from Parks Canada, is a desk for the **Banff/Lake Louise Tourism Bureau.** This organization represents businesses and commercial establishments in the park. Here you can find out about accommodations and restaurants, and have any other questions answered. To answer the most frequently asked question, the restrooms are downstairs. For general tourism information, contact the Banff/Lake Louise Tourism Bureau office (403/762-8421, www.banfflakelouise.com).

Newspapers

Look for the free *Crag and Canyon* each Tuesday. It's been keeping residents and visitors informed about park issues and town gossip for more than a century. The *Rocky Mountain Outlook* is another free weekly newspaper (Thursday) that offers coverage of mountain life and upcoming events. Both are available on stands at businesses throughout town.

Books and Bookstores

The Canadian Rockies are one of the most written about, and definitely the most photographed, regions in Canada. As a walk along Banff Avenue will confirm, there is definitely no lack of postcards, calendars, and books about the area.

Ted (E. J.) Hart, director of the Whyte Museum, has authored over a dozen books on the history of the park; these are sold at the Whyte Museum Bookstore. **Summerthought Publishing** (www.summerthought.com) is a local company that has been publishing the authoritative *Canadian Rockies Trail Guide* since 1971. Look for **Gem Trek** (www.gemtrek.com)

maps at bookstores and gift shops throughout Banff National Park.

The Bear and the Butterfly (214 Banff Ave., 403/762-8911, 9:30 A.M.–9:30 P.M. daily in summer, shorter hours the rest of the year), operated by the nonprofit Friends of Banff organization, holds a thoughtful selection of nature and recreation books. They also have a smaller store within the Banff Visitor Centre (224 Banff Ave., 403/762-8918). The **Whyte Museum Bookstore** (111 Bear St., 403/762-2291, 10 A.M.–5 P.M. daily) specializes in regional natural and human history.

Banff Public Library

Banff's library (opposite Central Park at 101 Bear St., 403/762-2661, 10 A.M.–8 P.M. Mon.–Thurs., 10 A.M.–6 P.M. Fri., 11 A.M.–6 P.M. Sat., and 1–5 P.M. Sun.) boasts an extensive collection of nonfiction books, many about the park and its environs, which makes it an excellent rainy-day hangout. It also has a large collection of magazines and newspapers. Internet access is free, but book ahead.

SERVICES

The **post office** (9 A.M.–5:30 P.M. Mon.–Fri.) is on the corner of Buffalo and Bear Streets opposite Central Park. The general-delivery service here is probably among the busiest in the country, with the thousands of seasonal workers in the area and no home mail-delivery service.

Major banks can be found along Banff Avenue and are generally open 10 A.M.–4 P.M. Mon.–Thurs. and 9 A.M.–4:30 P.M. Friday. The **Bank of Montreal** (107 Banff Ave., 403/762-2275) allows cash advances with MasterCard, while the **C.I.B.C.** (98 Banff Ave., 403/762-3317) accepts Visa. **Freya's Currency Exchange** is in the Clock Tower Mall (108 Banff Ave., 403/762-4652).

The only downtown laundry is **Cascade Coin Laundry** (7:30 A.M.–10 P.M. daily), on the lower level of the Cascade Plaza. **Chalet Coin Laundry** (8 A.M.–10 P.M. daily) is on Tunnel Mountain Road at the Douglas Fir Resort, within walking distance of all Tunnel Mountain accommodations.

Along Banff Avenue you'll find a handful of photo shops with digital imaging capabilities; check around for the cheapest because many have special offers. The most competitive and reliable is the **Banff Camera Shop** (101 Banff Ave., 403/762-3562).

Mineral Springs Hospital (301 Lynx St., 403/762-2222) has 24-hour emergency service. **Rexall Drug Store,** on the lower level of the Cascade Plaza (317 Banff Ave., 403/762-2245), is open until 9 P.M. daily.

Send and receive email and surf the Internet at the following Banff locations: **Banff Public Library** (101 Bear St., 403/762-2661, 10 A.M.–8 P.M. Mon.–Thurs., 10 A.M.–6 P.M. Fri., 11 A.M.–6 P.M. Sat., and 1–5 P.M. Sun.); **Cascade Plaza** (lower level, 315 Banff Ave, 403/762-8484, 7:30 A.M.–10 P.M. daily); **Cyberweb Internet Cafe** (Sundance Mall, 215 Banff Ave., 403/762-9226, 9 A.M.–midnight daily).

GETTING THERE
From Calgary International Airport
Calgary International Airport, 128 kilometers (80 miles) east, is the closest airport to Banff National Park. **Brewster** (403/762-6767 or 800/661-1152, www.brewster.ca) shuttles between the airport and Banff National Park twice daily, stopping at Banff, then continuing to Lake Louise. Calgary to Banff is adult $52, child $26. This shuttle delivers guests to all major Banff hotels as well as the **Brewster Tour and Transportation Centre,** a five-minute walk from downtown Banff at 100 Gopher Street. The depot has a ticket office, lockers, a café, and a gift shop. It's open 7:30 A.M.–10:45 P.M. daily. The other shuttle company is **Banff Airporter** (403/762-3330 or 888/449-2901, www.banffairporter.com), offering door-to-door service for around the same price. Adjacent desks at the airport's Arrivals level take bookings, but reserve a seat by booking over the phone or online in advance. The earliest service back to the airport departs Banff at 4:30 A.M.

Greyhound
Greyhound (403/762-1092 or 800/661-8747, www.greyhound.ca) offers scheduled service from the Calgary bus depot at 877 Greyhound Way SW, five times daily to the Banff Railway Station and Samson Mall, Lake Louise. Greyhound buses leave Vancouver from the depot at 1150 Station Street, three times daily for the scenic 14-hour ride to the park.

GETTING AROUND
Most of the sights and many trailheads are within walking distance of town. **Banff Transit** (403/760-8294) operates bus service along two routes through the town of Banff: one from the Fairmont Banff Springs to the RV and trailer parking area at the north end of Banff Avenue, the other from the Fairmont Banff Springs to the Tunnel Mountain campgrounds. Mid-May–September, buses run twice an hour between 7 A.M. and midnight. October–December, the two routes are merged as one, with buses running hourly midday–midnight. No local buses run the rest of the year. Travel costs $2 per sector.

Cabs around Banff are reasonably priced—flag drop is $4, then it's $2 per kilometer. From the Banff bus depot to Tunnel Mountain accommodations will run around $8, same to the Fairmont Banff Springs, more after midnight. Call **Banff Taxi** (403/762-4444).

The days when a row of horse-drawn buggies eagerly awaited the arrival of wealthy visitors at the CPR Station have long since passed, but the **Trail Rider Store** (132 Banff Ave., 403/762-4551) offers visitors rides around town in a beautifully restored carriage ($18 per person for 15 minutes). Expect to pay $32 per carriage for a short loop along the Bow River.

Car Rental
Plan on renting a vehicle before you reach the park. In addition to high pricing for walk-in customers, the main catch is that no local companies offer unlimited mileage. The most you'll get is a free 150 kilometers (93 miles), and then expect to pay 25 cents per kilometer thereafter. Agencies and their local contact numbers are: **Avis** (Cascade Plaza, 317 Banff Ave., 403/762-3222), **Budget** (Brewster's Mountain

PARKING PROBLEMS (AND HOW TO AVOID THEM)

The downtown core of Banff is busy year-round, but especially so between late June and early September after 10 A.M. If you're staying in a motel along Banff Avenue or on Tunnel Mountain, don't drive into town – walk or catch a Banff Transit bus (ask at your accommodation for a schedule).

If you do drive into downtown, don't let not finding a parking spot on Banff Avenue ruin your holiday. Head to the parking garage at the corner of Bear and Lynx Streets, cross the Bow River and park in recreation grounds, or cruise for a space along Lynx or Beaver Street.

For travelers with RVs or trailers, finding a downtown parking spot can be a challenge. If you're planning on staying at one of the campgrounds on Tunnel Mountain, check in first, then walk or catch the Banff Transit bus (it departs the campground every 30 minutes; $2) to downtown. On the northeast side of town, signposted off Banff Avenue, is an RV parking/trailer drop-off lot. From here Banff Transit buses run every 30 minutes to downtown. If you must bring your rig in town and the few RV-only parking spots at the corner of Lynx and Wolf Streets are taken, there are no options other than the suggestions I give above for regular vehicles.

© ANDREW HEMPSTEAD

Murals of wild animals make public transit buses in Banff very distinctive.

Lodge, 208 Caribou St., 403/762-4565), **Hertz** (Fairmont Banff Springs, Spray Ave., 403/762-2027), and **National** (corner of Lynx and Caribou Streets, 403/762-2688). Reservations for vehicles in Banff should be made well in advance, especially in July and August.

Persons with Disabilities

The Banff and Lake Louise Visitor Centres are wheelchair accessible—restrooms, information desks, and theater are all barrier free. Once inside, use the handy Touchsource monitors for a full listing of all barrier-free services within the park. An all-terrain wheelchair is available at the Cave and Basin National Historic Site for use on park trails. To reserve, call 403/762-1566.

Lake Louise and Vicinity

Lake Louise is 56 kilometers (35 miles) northwest of Banff along the TransCanada Highway, or a little bit longer if you take the quieter Bow Valley Parkway. The hamlet of Lake Louise, composed of a small mall, hotels, and restaurants, is in the Bow Valley, just west of the TransCanada Highway. The lake itself is 200 vertical meters (660 vertical feet) above the valley floor, along a winding four-kilometer (2.5-mile) road. Across the valley is Canada's second-largest winter resort, also called Lake Louise. It's a world-class facility renowned for diverse terrain, abundant snow, and breathtaking views.

When you see the first flush of morning sun hit Victoria Glacier, and the impossibly steep northern face of Mount Victoria reflected in the sparkling, emerald green waters of Lake Louise, you'll understand why this lake is regarded as one of the world's seven natural wonders. Overlooking the magnificent scene, Fairmont Chateau Lake Louise is without a doubt one of the world's most photographed hotels. Apart from staring, photographing, and videotaping, the area has plenty to keep you busy. Nearby you'll find some of the park's best hiking, canoeing, and horseback riding. Only a short distance away is Moraine Lake, not as famous as Lake Louise but rivaling it in beauty.

From Lake Louise the TransCanada Highway continues west, exiting the park over Kicking Horse Pass (1,647 meters/5,400 feet) and passing through Yoho National Park to Golden. Highway 93, the famous Icefields Parkway, begins one kilometer (0.6 mile) north of the village and heads northwest through the park's northern reaches to Jasper National Park.

SIGHTS
◖ Lake Louise

In summer, about 10,000 visitors per day make the journey from the Bow Valley floor up to Lake Louise. By noon the tiered parking lot is

"LAKE OF LITTLE FISHES"

During the summer of 1882, Tom Wilson, an outfitter, was camped near the confluence of the Bow and Pipestone Rivers when he heard the distant rumblings of an avalanche. He questioned Stoney Indian guides and was told the noises originated from the "Lake of Little Fishes." The following day, Wilson, led by a native guide, hiked to the lake to investigate. He became the first white man to lay eyes on what he named Emerald Lake. Two years later, the name was changed to Lake Louise, honoring Princess Louise Caroline Alberta, daughter of Queen Victoria.

A railway station known as Laggan was built where the rail line passed closest to the lake, six kilometers (3.7 miles) away. Until a road was completed in 1926, everyone arrived by train. The station's name was changed to Lake Louise in 1913 to prevent confusion among visitors. In 1890, a modest two-bedroom wooden hotel replaced a crude cabin that had been built on the shore of the lake as word of its beauty spread. After many additions, a disastrous fire, and the addition of a concrete wing in 1925, the château of today took shape, minus a convention center that opened in 2004.

Lake Louise

© ANDREW HEMPSTEAD

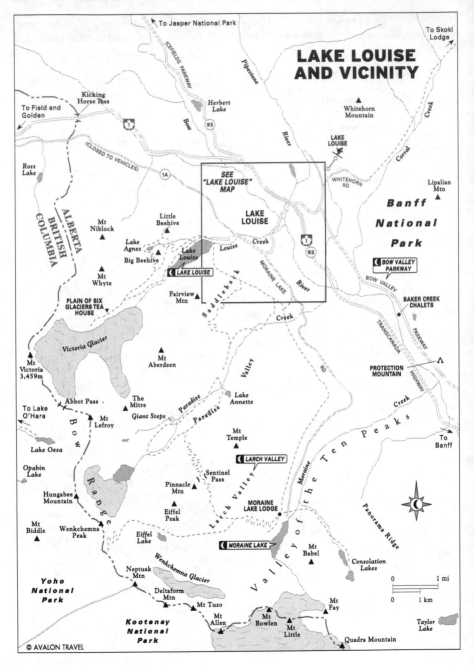

LAKE LOUISE AND VICINITY

To Jasper National Park

To Skoki Lodge

ICEFIELDS PARKWAY

Pipestone

Kicking Horse Pass

To Field and Golden

Herbert Lake

Whitehorn Mountain

Creek

Bow

93

River

LAKE LOUISE

1

(CLOSED TO VEHICLES)

Ross Lake

1A

SEE "LAKE LOUISE" MAP

WHITEHORN RD

Lipalian Mtn

Banff

National

Park

ALBERTA

BRITISH COLUMBIA

Mt Niblock

Little Beehive

LAKE LOUISE

Lake Agnes

Big Beehive

Lake Louise

Louise

Creek

1

93

BOW VALLEY PARKWAY

Mt Whyte

🚶 LAKE LOUISE

Saddleback

MORAINE LAKE

BOW VALLEY

River

BAKER CREEK CHALETS

PLAIN OF SIX GLACIERS TEA HOUSE

Fairview Mtn

Creek

TRANS-CANADA

PARKWAY

Victoria Glacier

Mt Aberdeen

Valley

PROTECTION MOUNTAIN

HIGHWAY

Mt Victoria 3,459m

Abbot Pass

The Mitre

Paradise

Lake Annette

RD

To Lake O'Hara

Mt Lefroy

Giant Steps

Paradise

Mt Temple

Peaks

To Banff

Lake Oesa

Bow

🚶 LARCH VALLEY

Ten

Creek

Opabin Lake

Range

Sentinel Pass

the

Hungabee Mountain

Pinnacle Mtn

Larch Valley

of

Mt Biddle

Wenkchemna Peak

Eiffel Peak

MORAINE LAKE LODGE

Valley

Panorama Ridge

Eiffel Lake

🚶 MORAINE LAKE

Mt Babel

Consolation Lakes

Wenkchemna Glacier

Yoho National Park

Neptuak Mtn

0   1 mi

0   1 km

Deltaform Mtn

Mt Tuzo

Kootenay National Park

Mt Allen

Mt Bowlen

Mt Fay

Mt Little

Taylor Lake

Quadra Mountain

© AVALON TRAVEL

often full. An alternative to the road is one of two hiking trails that begin in the village and end at the public parking lot. From here several paved trails lead to the lake's eastern shore. From these vantage points the dramatic setting can be fully appreciated. The lake is 2.4 kilometers (1.5 miles) long, 500 meters (1,640 feet) wide, and up to 90 meters (295 feet) deep. Its cold waters reach a maximum temperature of 4°C (39°F) in August.

Fairmont Chateau Lake Louise is a tourist attraction in itself. Built by the CPR to take the pressure off the popular Banff Springs Resort, the château has seen many changes in the last 100 years, yet it remains one of the world's great mountain resorts. No one minds the hordes of camera-toting tourists who traipse

through each day—and there's really no way to avoid them. The immaculately manicured gardens between the château and the lake make an interesting foreground for the millions of Lake Louise photographs taken each year. At the lakeshore boathouse, canoes are rented for $40 per hour.

The snow-covered peak at the back of the lake is **Mount Victoria** (3,459 meters/11,350 feet), which sits on the Continental Divide. Amazingly, its base is more than 10 kilometers (6.2 miles) from the eastern end of the lake. Mount Victoria, first climbed in 1897, remains one of the park's most popular peaks for mountaineers. Although the difficult northeast face (facing the château) was first successfully ascended in 1922, the most popular and easiest

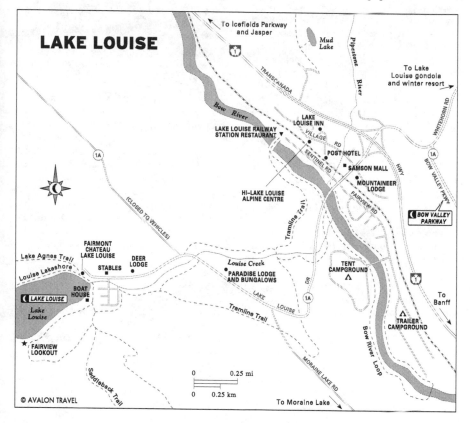

route to the summit is along the southeast ridge, approached from Abbot Pass.

Moraine Lake

Although less than half the size of Lake Louise, Moraine Lake is just as spectacular and worthy of just as much film. It is up a winding road 13 kilometers (eight miles) off Lake Louise Drive. Its rugged setting, nestled in the Valley of the Ten Peaks among the towering mountains of the main ranges, has provided inspiration for millions of people from around the world since Walter Wilcox became the first white man to reach its shore in 1899. Wilcox's subsequent writings—such as "no scene has given me an equal impression of inspiring solitude and rugged grandeur"—guaranteed the lake's future popularity. Although Wilcox was a knowledgeable man, he named the lake on the assumption that it was dammed by a glacial moraine deposited by the retreating Wenkchemna Glacier. In fact, the large rock pile that blocks its waters was deposited by major rockfalls from the Tower of Babel to the south. The lake often remains frozen until June, and the access road is closed all winter. A trail leads along the lake's northern shore, and canoes are rented for $30 per hour from the concession below the lodge.

Sightseeing Gondola

During summer the main ski lift at Lake Louise winter resort (403/522-3555) whisks visitors up the face of Mount Whitehorn to Whitehorn Lodge in either open chairs or enclosed gondola cars. The view from the top—at an altitude of more than two kilometers (1.2 miles) above sea level across the Bow Valley, Lake Louise, and the Continental Divide—is among the most spectacular in the Canadian Rockies. Short trails lead through the forests, across open meadows, and, for the energetic, to the summit of Mount Whitehorn, more than 600 vertical meters (1,970 vertical feet) above. Visitors are free to walk these trails, but it pays to join a guided walk ($5) if you'd like to learn about the surrounding environment. After working up an appetite (and working off breakfast), head to the teahouse in the

© ANDREW HEMPSTEAD

After a gondola ride, relax in the impressive Lodge of the Ten Peaks.

Whitehorn Lodge, try the outdoor barbecue, or, back at the base area, enjoy lunch at the **Lodge of the Ten Peaks,** the resort's impressive post-and-beam day lodge. The lift operates 9 A.M.–4 P.M. daily May–September, with extended summer hours of 9 A.M.–5 P.M.; adult $26, child $13. Ride-and-dine packages are an excellent deal. Pay an extra $3 per person and have a buffet breakfast (8–11 A.M.) included with the gondola ride or $7 extra for the buffet lunch (11:30 A.M.–2:30 P.M.). Free shuttles run from Lake Louise accommodations to the day lodge.

HIKING

The variety of hiking opportunities in the vicinity of Lake Louise and Moraine Lake is surely equal to any area on the face of the earth. The region's potential for outdoor recreation was first realized in the late 1800s, and it soon became the center of hiking activity in the Canadian Rockies. This popularity continues today; trails here are among the most heavily used in the park. Hiking is best early or late in the short summer season. Head out early in the morning to miss the strollers, high heels, dogs, and bear bells that you'll surely encounter during the busiest periods.

The two main trailheads are at Fairmont Chateau Lake Louise and Moraine Lake. Two trails lead from the village to the château (a pleasant alternative to driving the steep and busy Lake Louise Drive). Shortest is the 2.7-kilometer/1.7-mile **Louise Creek Trail.** It begins on the downstream side of the point where Lake Louise Drive crosses the Bow River, crosses Louise Creek three times, and ends at the Lake Louise parking lot. The other trail, **Tramline,** is 4.5 kilometers (2.8 miles) longer but not as steep. It begins behind the railway station and follows the route of a narrow-gauge railway that once transported guests from the CPR line to Chateau Lake Louise.

Bow River Loop

- Length: 7 kilometers/4.3 miles (1.5–2 hours)
- Elevation gain: minimal
- Rating: easy
- Trailheads: various points throughout Lake Louise Village, including behind Samson Mall

This loop follows both banks of the Bow River southeast from the railway station. Used by joggers and cyclists to access various points in the village, the trail also links the station to the Lake Louise Alpine Centre, Post Hotel, Samson Mall, both campgrounds, and the Louise Creek and Tramline trails to Lake Louise. Interpretive signs along its length provide information on the Bow River ecosystem.

Louise Lakeshore

- Length: 2 kilometers/1.2 miles (30 minutes) one-way
- Elevation gain: none
- Rating: easy
- Trailhead: Lake Louise, 4 kilometers (2.5 miles) from TransCanada Highway

Probably the busiest trail in all of the Canadian Rockies, this one follows the north shore of Lake Louise from in front of the château to the west end of the lake. Here numerous braided glacial streams empty their silt-filled waters into Lake Louise. Along the trail's length are benches for sitting and pondering what English mountaineer James Outram once described as "a gem of composition and of coloring? perhaps unrivalled anywhere."

Plain of the Six Glaciers

- Length: 5.3 kilometers/3.3 miles (90 minutes) one-way
- Elevation gain: 370 meters/1,215 feet
- Rating: easy/moderate
- Trailhead: Lake Louise

Hikers along this trail are rewarded not only with panoramic views of the glaciated peaks of the main range, but also with a rustic trail's-end teahouse serving homemade goodies baked on a wooden stove. For the first two kilometers (1.2

Plain of the Six Glaciers teahouse

© ANDREW HEMPSTEAD

miles), the trail follows Louise Lakeshore Trail to the western end of the lake. From there it begins a steady climb through a forest of spruce and subalpine fir. It enters an open area where an avalanche has come tumbling down (now a colorful carpet of wildflowers), then passes through a forested area into a vast wasteland of moraines produced by the advance and retreat of Victoria Glacier. Views of surrounding peaks continue to improve until the trail enters a stunted forest. After switchbacking up through this forest, the trail arrives at the teahouse.

Built by the CPR at the turn of the 20th century, the teahouse operates the same way now as it did then. Supplies are packed in by horse, and all cooking is done in a rustic kitchen. It's open July through early September.

After resting, continue one kilometer (0.6 mile) to the end of the trail on the narrow top of a lateral moraine. From here the trail's namesakes are visible. From left to right the glaciers are Aberdeen, Upper Lefroy, Lower Lefroy, Upper Victoria, Lower Victoria, and Pope's. Between Mount Lefroy (3,441 meters/11,290 feet) and Mount Victoria (3,459 meters/11,350 feet) is Abbot Pass, where it's possible to make out Abbot Hut on the skyline. When constructed in 1922, this stone structure was the highest building in Canada. The pass and hut are named for Phillip Abbot, who died attempting to climb Mount Lefroy in 1896.

Lake Agnes

- Length: 3.6 kilometers/2.2 miles (90 minutes) one-way
- Elevation gain: 400 meters/1,312 feet
- Rating: moderate
- Trailhead: Lake Louise

This moderately strenuous hike is one of the park's most popular. It begins in front of the château, branching right near the beginning of the Louise Lakeshore Trail. For the first 2.5 kilometers (1.6 miles), the trail climbs steeply, switchbacking through a forest of subalpine fir and Engelmann spruce, crossing a horse trail, passing a lookout, and leveling out at tiny

Mirror Lake. Here the old, traditional trail veers right (use it if the ground is wet or snowy), while a more direct route veers left to the Plain of the Six Glaciers. The final elevation gain along both trails is made easier by a flight of steps beside Bridal Veil Falls. The trail ends beside a rustic teahouse overlooking Lake Agnes, a subalpine lake nestled in a hanging valley. The teahouse offers homemade soups, healthy sandwiches, and a wide assortment of teas.

From the teahouse a one-kilometer (0.6-mile) trail leads to Little Beehive and impressive views of the Bow Valley. Another trail leads around the northern shore of Lake Agnes, climbing to Big Beehive or joining to the Plain of the Six Glaciers Trail, just 3.2 kilometers (two miles) from the château and 2.1 kilometers (1.3 miles) from the teahouse at the end of that trail.

Big Beehive

- Length: 5 kilometers/3.1 miles (2 hours) one-way
- Elevation gain: 520 meters/1,710 feet
- Rating: moderate
- Trailhead: Lake Louise

The lookout atop the larger of the two "beehives" is one of the best places to admire the uniquely colored waters of Lake Louise, more than 500 meters (1,640 feet) directly below. The various trails to the summit have one thing in common—all are steep. But the rewards are worth every drop of sweat along the way. The most popular route follows the Lake Agnes Trail for the first 3.6 kilometers (2.2 miles) to Lake Agnes. From the teahouse, a trail leads to the western end of the lake, then switchbacks steeply up an exposed north-facing ridge. At the crest of the ridge, the trail forks. To the right it descends to the Plain of the Six Glaciers Trail; to the left it continues 300 meters (0.2 mile) to a log gazebo. This trail is not well defined, but scrambling through the large boulders is easy. Across Lake Louise is Fairview Mountain (2,745 meters/9,000 feet), and behind this peak is the distinctive shape of Mount Temple (3,549 meters/11,645 feet). Views also extend up the lake to Mount Lefroy and northeast to Lake Louise winter resort. Views from the edge of the cliff are spectacular, but be very careful—it's a long, long way down. By returning down the Lake Louise side of the Big Beehive, the loop is 11.5 kilometers (7.1 miles).

it +?
top

X Saddleback *Not Trisha*

- Length: 3.7 kilometers/2.3 miles (90 minutes) one-way
- Elevation gain: 600 meters/1,970 feet
- Rating: moderate
- Trailhead: boathouse, Lake Louise

This trail climbs the lower slopes of Fairview Mountain from beside the boathouse on Lake Louise, ending in an alpine meadow with a view of Mount Temple from across Paradise Valley. Four hundred meters (0.2 mile) from the trailhead, the trail forks. Keep left and follow the steep switchbacks through a forest of Engelmann spruce and subalpine fir until reaching the flower-filled meadow. The meadow is actually a pass between Fairview Mountain (to the northwest) and Saddle Mountain (to the southeast). Although most hikers are content with the awesome views from the pass and return along the same trail, it is possible to continue to the summit of Fairview (2,745 meters/9,000 feet), a further climb of 400 vertical meters (1,310 vertical feet). The barely discernible, switchbacking trail to the summit begins near a stand of larch trees above the crest of Saddleback. As you would expect, the view from the top is stupendous; Lake Louise is more than one kilometer (0.6 mile) directly below. This option is for strong, experienced hikers only. From the Saddleback, the trail descends into Sheol Valley, then into Paradise Valley. The entire loop would be 15 kilometers (9.3 miles).

Paradise Valley

- Length: 18 kilometers/11.2 miles (6 hours) round-trip

- Elevation gain: 380 meters/1,250 feet
- Rating: moderate
- Trailhead: Moraine Lake Road, 3.5 kilometers (2.2 miles) from Lake Louise Drive

This aptly named trail makes for a long day hike, but it can be broken up by overnighting at the backcountry campground at the far end of the loop. The trail climbs steadily for the first five kilometers (3.1 miles), crossing Paradise Creek numerous times and passing the junction of a trail that climbs the Sheol Valley to Saddleback. After five kilometers (3.1 miles) the trail divides again, following either side of the valley to form a 13-kilometer (eight-mile) loop. **Lake Annette** is 700 meters (0.4 mile) along the left fork. It's a typical subalpine lake in a unique setting—nestled against the near-vertical 1,200-meter (3,940-foot) north face of snow- and ice-capped **Mount Temple** (3,549 meters/11,645 feet), one of the 10 highest peaks in the Canadian Rockies. This difficult face was successfully climbed in 1966, relatively late for mountaineering firsts. The lake is a worthy destination in itself. Allow yourself four hours round-trip from the trailhead. For those completing the entire loop, continue beyond the lake into an open avalanche area that affords views across Paradise Valley. Look and listen for pikas and marmots among the boulders. The trail then passes through Horseshoe Meadow, crosses Paradise Creek, and heads back down the valley. Keep to the left at all trail crossings, and you'll quickly arrive at a series of waterfalls known as the Giant Steps. From the base of these falls, it is eight kilometers (five miles) back to the trailhead.

◖ Larch Valley

- Length: 2.9 kilometers/1.8 miles (60 minutes) one-way
- Elevation gain: 400 meters/1,310 feet
- Rating: moderate
- Trailhead: Moraine Lake, 13 kilometers (8 miles) from Lake Louise Drive

In fall, when the larch trees have turned a

magnificent gold and the sun is shining, few spots in the Canadian Rockies can match the beauty of this valley, but don't expect to find much solitude (and don't be too disappointed if the trail is closed in fall—it often is because of wildlife). Although the most popular time for visiting the valley is fall, it is a worthy destination all summer, when the open meadows are filled with colorful wildflowers. The trail begins just past Moraine Lake Lodge and climbs fairly steeply, with occasional glimpses of Moraine Lake below. After reaching the junction of the Eiffel Lake Trail, keep right, passing through an open forest of larch and into the meadow beyond. The range of larch is restricted within the park, and this is one of the few areas where they are prolific. Mount Fay (3,235 meters/10,615 feet) is the dominant peak on the skyline, rising above the other mountains that make up the Valley of the Ten Peaks.

Sentinel Pass

- Length: 5.8 kilometers/3.6 miles (2–3 hours) one-way
- Elevation gain: 725 meters/2,380 feet
- Rating: moderate/difficult
- Trailhead: Moraine Lake

Keen hikers should consider continuing through the open meadows of Larch Valley to Sentinel Pass (2,608 meters/8,560 feet), one of the park's highest trail-accessible passes. The length and elevation gain listed are from Moraine Lake. Once in Larch Valley, you're halfway there and have made over half of the elevation gain. Upon reaching Larch Valley, take the formed trail that winds through the open meadow. After climbing steadily beyond Minnestimma Lakes, the trail switchbacks for 1.2 kilometers (0.7 mile) up a steep scree slope to the pass, sandwiched between Pinnacle Mountain (3,067 meters/10,060 feet) and Mount Temple (3,549 meters/11,645 feet). From the pass most hikers opt to return along the same trail, although with advanced planning it is possible to continue into Paradise

Valley and back to the Moraine Lake access road, a total of 17 kilometers (10.6 miles) one-way.

Eiffel Lake

- Length: 5.6 kilometers/3.5 miles (2 hours) one-way
- Elevation gain: 400 meters/1,310 feet
- Rating: moderate/difficult
- Trailhead: Moraine Lake

Eiffel Lake is small, and it looks even smaller in its rugged and desolate setting, surrounded by the famed Valley of the Ten Peaks. For the first 2.4 kilometers (1.5 miles), follow the Larch Valley Trail, then fork left. Most of the elevation gain has already been made, and the trail remains relatively level before emerging onto an open slope from where each of the 10 peaks can be seen, along with Moraine Lake far below. From left to right the peaks are Fay, Little, Bowlen, Perren, Septa, Allen, Tuzo, Deltaform, Neptuak, and Wenkchemna. The final two peaks are divided by Wenkchemna Pass (2,605 meters/8,550 feet), a further four kilometers (2.5 miles) and 360 vertical meters (1,180 vertical feet) above Eiffel Lake. The lake itself soon comes into view. It lies in a depression formed by a rock slide from Neptuak Mountain. The lake is named for **Eiffel Peak** (3,085 meters/10,120 feet), a rock pinnacle behind it, which with a little imagination could be compared to the Eiffel Tower in Paris.

Consolation Lakes

- Length: 3 kilometers/1.9 miles (1 hour) one-way
- Elevation gain: 65 meters/213 feet
- Rating: easy/moderate
- Trailhead: beside the restrooms at Moraine Lake parking lot

This short trail begins with a crossing of Moraine Creek at the outlet of Moraine Lake and ends at a pleasant subalpine lake. The first section of the trail traverses a boulder-strewn rock pile—the result of rock slides on the imposing Tower of Babel (3,100 meters/10,170 feet)—before entering a dense forest of Engelmann spruce and subalpine fir and following Babel Creek to the lower lake. The wide valley affords 360-degree views of the surrounding jagged peaks, including Mount Temple back down the valley and Mounts Bident and Quandra at the far end of the lakes.

Skoki Lodge

- Length: 14.4 kilometers/8.9 miles (5 hours) one-way
- Elevation gain: 775 meters/2,540 feet
- Rating: moderate/difficult
- Trailhead: end of Fish Creek Road, off Whitehorn Road 1.8 kilometers (1.1 miles) north of Lake Louise interchange

The trail into historic Skoki Lodge is only one of the endless hiking opportunities tucked behind Lake Louise winter resort, across the valley from all hikes detailed previously. The first four kilometers (2.5 miles) of the trail are along a gravel access road leading to Temple Lodge, part of the Lake Louise winter resort. From here, the trail climbs to Boulder Pass, passing a campground and Halfway Hut, above Corral Creek. The pass harbors a large population of pikas and hoary marmots. The trail then follows the north shore of Ptarmigan Lake before climbing again to Deception Pass, named for its false summit. It then descends into Skoki Valley, passing the Skoki Lakes and eventually reaching Skoki Lodge. Just over one kilometer (0.6 mile) beyond the lodge is a campground, an excellent base for exploring the region.

OTHER SUMMER RECREATION

In Lake Louise, "summer fun" means hiking—and lots of it. You may see small fish swimming along the shore of Lake Louise, but the fishing in this lake and all others in the area is poor due to the super-cold glacial water. Talking of cold water, everyone is invited to take a swim in Lake Louise to celebrate the country's national holiday, **Canada Day** (July 1). You don't need to be Canadian to join in—just brave.

Through summer, **Brewster Lake Louise Stables** (403/522-3511) offers two-hour horseback rides to the end of **Lake Louise** for $72, half-day rides to **Lake Agnes Teahouse** for $115, and all-day rides up **Paradise Valley,** including lunch, for $270.

WINTER RECREATION

Lake Louise is an immense winter playground offering one of the world's premier alpine resorts, unlimited cross-country skiing, ice-skating, sleigh rides, and nearby heli-skiing. Between November and May, accommodation prices are reduced by up to 70 percent (except Christmas holidays). Lift and lodging packages begin at $80 per person, and you'll always be able to get a table at your favorite restaurant.

Lake Louise Resort

Canada's answer to U.S. megaresorts such as Vail and Killington is Lake Louise (403/522-3555 or 877/253-6888, www.skilouise.com), which opens in November and operates until mid-May. The nation's second-largest winter resort (behind only Whistler/Blackcomb) comprises 1,700 hectares (4,200 acres) of gentle trails, mogul fields, long cruising runs, steep chutes, and vast bowls filled with famous Rocky Mountain powder.

The resort is made up of four distinct faces. The front side has a vertical drop of 1,000 meters (3,280 feet) and is served by eight lifts, including four high-speed quads, and western Canada's only six-passenger chairlift. Resort statistics are impressive: a 990-meter (3,250-foot) vertical rise, 1,700 hectares (4,200 acres) of patrolled terrain, and more than 100 named runs. The four back bowls are each as big as many midsize resorts and are all well above the tree line. Larch and Ptarmigan faces have a variety of terrain, allowing you to follow the sun as it moves across the sky or escape into trees for protection on windy days. Each of the three day lodges has a restaurant and bar. Ski

playing pond hockey in front of the Fairmont Chateau Lake Louise

© ANDREW HEMPSTEAD

and snowboard rentals, clothing, and souvenirs are available in the Lodge of the Ten Peaks, a magnificent post-and-beam day lodge that overlooks the front face.

Lift tickets per day are adult $79, senior $65, youth $54, and child younger than 12 $23. Free guided tours of the mountain are available three times daily—inquire at customer service. Free shuttle buses run regularly from Lake Louise accommodations to the hill. From Banff you pay $15 round-trip for transportation to Lake Louise. For information on packages and multiday tickets that cover all three park resorts, go to www.skibig3.com.

Cross-Country Skiing

The most popular cross-country skiing areas are on Lake Louise, along Moraine Lake Road, and in Skoki Valley at the back of the Lake Louise ski area. For details and helpful trail classifications, pick up a copy of *Cross-Country Skiing–Nordic Trails in Banff National Park,* from the Lake Louise Visitor Centre. Before heading out, check the weather forecast at the visitors center or call 403/762-2088. For avalanche reports, call 403/762-1460.

Ice-Skating and Sleigh Rides

Of all the ice-skating rinks in Canada, the one on frozen Lake Louise, in front of the château, is surely the most spectacular. Spotlights allow skating after dark, and on special occasions hot chocolate is served. Skates are available in the château at **Chateau Mountain Sports** (403/522-3628); $9 for two hours.

Brewster Lake Louise Sleigh Rides (403/522-3511) offers rides in traditional horse-drawn sleighs along the shores of Lake Louise beginning from in front of the château. Although blankets are supplied, you should still bundle up. The one-hour ride is $28 per person, $18 for children. Reservations are necessary. The rides are scheduled hourly from 11 A.M. on weekends, from 3 P.M. weekdays, with the last ride between 6 and 9 P.M.

NIGHTLIFE

The lounge in the **Post Hotel** (200 Pipestone Dr., 403/522-3989) oozes mountain style and upscale charm. It's cozy, quiet, and the perfect place to relax in front of a fire with a cocktail before moving on to the adjacent fine-dining restaurant. Not your scene? Hang out with seasonal workers at the smoky **Lake Louise Grill & Bar** (upstairs in Samson Mall, 403/522-3879), then move across the road with your newfound friends to **Charlie's Pub** (Lake Louise Inn, 403/522-3791) for dancing to recorded music until 2 A.M. Up at the Fairmont Chateau Lake Louise (403/522-3511) is **The Glacier Saloon** (from 6 P.M. daily), where on most summer nights a DJ plays music ranging from pop to western.

ACCOMMODATIONS AND CAMPING

In summer, accommodations at Lake Louise are even harder to come by than in Banff, so it's essential to make reservations well in advance. Any rooms not taken by early afternoon will be the expensive ones.

Under $50

With beds for $100 less than anyplace else in the village, the 164-bed **HI-Lake Louise Alpine Centre** (403/522-2200 or 866/762-4122, www.hihostels.ca) is understandably popular. Of log construction, with large windows and high vaulted ceilings, the lodge is a joint venture between the Alpine Club of Canada and the Hostelling International Canada. Beyond the reception area is **Bill Peyto's Cafe**, the least expensive place to eat in Lake Louise. Upstairs is a large timber-frame lounge area and guide's room—a quiet place to plan your next hike or browse through the large collection of mountain literature. Other amenities include Wi-Fi Internet, a laundry, games room, and wintertime ski shuttle. Members of Hostelling International pay $38 per person per night (nonmembers $42) for a dorm bed or $109 s or d ($119 for nonmembers) in a private room. Rates are discounted to $30 for a dorm and $82 s or d for a private room ($35 and $92, respectively, for nonmembers) October–May, including throughout the extremely busy winter season. The hostel is open year-round, with check-in after 3 P.M. In summer and on weekends during the winter season, advance bookings (up to six months) are essential. The hostel is on Village Road, less than one kilometer (0.6 mile) from Samson Mall.

$150-200

An excellent option for families and those looking for old fashioned mountain charm is ◖ **Paradise Lodge and Bungalows** (403/522-3595, www.paradiselodge.com, mid-May–early Oct., $215–345 s or d). This family-operated lodge provides excellent value in a wonderfully tranquil setting. Spread out around well-manicured gardens are 21 attractive cabins in four configurations. Each has a rustic, yet warm and inviting interior, with comfortable beds, a separate sitting area, and an en suite bathroom. Each cabin has a small fridge, microwave, and coffeemaker, while the larger ones have full kitchens and separate bedrooms. Instead of television, children are kept happy with a playground that includes a sandbox and jungle gym. On Wednesday and Sunday nights, a local naturalist presents an outdoor interpretive program for interested guests. The least-expensive cabins—complete with a classic cast-iron stove/fireplace combo—are $245 s or d, or pay $265 for a cabin with a big deck and soaring valley views. Twenty-four luxury suites, each with a fireplace, TV, one or two bedrooms, and fabulous mountain views, start at $290, or $325 with a kitchen. The Temple Suite, with all of the above as well as a large hot tub, is $345. To get there from the valley floor, follow Lake Louise Drive toward the Fairmont Chateau Lake Louise for three kilometers (1.9 miles); the lake itself is just one kilometer (0.6 mile) farther up the hill.

Historic **Deer Lodge** (403/410-7417 or 800/661-1595, www.crmr.com, $175–275 s or d) began life in 1921 as a teahouse, with rooms added in 1925. Facilities include a rooftop hot tub with glacier views, game room, restaurant (breakfast and dinner), and bar. The least-expensive rooms are older and don't have phones. Rooms in the $200–250 range are considerably larger, or pay $275 for a heritage-themed Tower Room. Deer Lodge is along Lake Louise Drive, up the hill from the village, and just a five-minute walk from the lake itself.

On the valley floor, **Mountaineer Lodge** (101 Village Rd., 403/522-3844, www.mountaineerlodge.com, May–mid-Oct., $189–239 s or d) offers large, functional guest rooms, many with mountain views and all with Wi-Fi Internet access. On the downside, the rooms have no phones or air-conditioning, and there is no elevator. Rates are halved during the first and last months of the operating season.

$200-250

Aside from the château, the **Lake Louise Inn** (210 Village Rd., 403/522-3791 or 800/661-9237, www.lakelouiseinn.com, from $220 s or d) is the village's largest lodging, with more than 200 units spread throughout five buildings. Across from the lobby, in the main lodge, is a gift shop and an activities desk, and beyond is a pizzeria, a restaurant, a bar, and an indoor pool. Most rates booked online include breakfast.

Over $250

Originally called Lake Louise Ski Lodge, the **⟨ Post Hotel** (200 Pipestone Dr., 403/522-3989 or 800/661-1586, www.posthotel.com, $345–455 s or d) is one of only a handful of Canadian accommodations that have

been accepted into the prestigious Relaix & Châteaux organization. Bordered to the east and south by the Pipestone River, it may lack views of Lake Louise, but it is as elegant, in a modern, woodsy way, as the château. Each bungalow-style room is furnished with Canadian pine and has a balcony. Many rooms have whirlpools and fireplaces, while some have kitchens. Other facilities include the upscale Temple Mountain Spa, an indoor pool, a steam room, and a library. The hotel has 17 different room types, with 26 different rates depending on the view. Between the main lodge and the Pipestone River are four sought-after cabins, each with a wood-burning fireplace; from $390 s or d.

At the lake for which it's named, four kilometers (2.5 miles) from the valley floor, is super-luxurious **Moraine Lake Lodge** (403/522-3733 or 877/522-2777, www.morainelake.com, June–Sept., $375–475 s or d). Designed by renowned architect Arthur Erickson, the lodge is a bastion of understated charm, partially obscured from the masses of day-trippers who visit the lake and yet taking

Post Hotel

© ANDREW HEMPSTEAD

full advantage of its location beside one of the world's most-photographed lakes. The decor reflects the wilderness location, with an abundance of polished log work and solid, practical furnishings in heritage-themed rooms. The rooms have no TVs or phones; instead guests take guided nature walks, have unlimited use of canoes, and are pampered with complimentary afternoon tea.

The famously fabulous **Fairmont Chateau Lake Louise** (403/522-3511 or 800/257-7544, www.fairmont.com), a historic 500-room hotel on the shore of Lake Louise, has views equal to any mountain resort in the world. But all this historic charm and mountain scenery comes at a price. During the summer season (late June–mid-October), the rack rate for rooms *without* a lake view is $659 s or d, while those with a view are $829. Rooms on the Fairmont Gold Floor come with a private concierge and upgraded everything for a little over $1,000. As at the company's sister property in Banff, most guests book a room as part of a package, either online at www.fairmont.com or through a travel agent, and end up

© ANDREW HEMPSTEAD

Fairmont Chateau Lake Louise

paying closer to $400 for a room in peak summer season. Official rates drop as low as $250 s or d outside of summer, with accommodation and ski pass packages often advertised for around $250 d. Children younger than 18 sharing with parents are free, but if you bring a pet, it'll be an extra $25.

Backcountry Accommodations

If you're prepared to lace up your hiking boots for a true mountain experience, consider spending time at █ **Skoki Lodge** (403/256-8473 or 800/258-7669, www.skoki.com, from $194 pp), north of the Lake Louise ski resort and far from the nearest road. Getting there requires an 11-kilometer (6.8-mile) hike or ski, depending on the season. The lodge is an excellent base for exploring nearby valleys and mountains. It dates to 1931, when it operated as a lodge for local Banff skiers, and is now a National Historic Site. Today it comprises a main lodge, sleeping cabins, and a wood-fired sauna. Accommodations are rustic   propane heat but no electricity—but comfortable, with mostly twin beds in the main lodge and cabins that sleep up to five. Rates include three meals daily, including a picnic lunch that guests build from a buffet-style layout before heading out hiking or skiing. The dining room and lounge center on a wood-burning fire, where guests come together each evening to swap tales from the trail and mingle with the convivial hosts. The operating season is mid-June–mid-October and mid-December–mid-April.

Campgrounds

Exit the TransCanada Highway at the Lake Louise interchange, 56 kilometers (35 miles) northwest of Banff, and take the first left beyond Samson Mall and under the railway bridge to reach **Lake Louise Campground,** within easy walking distance of the village. The campground is divided into two sections by the Bow River but is linked by the Bow River Loop hiking trail that leads into the village along either side of the Bow River. Individual sites throughout are close together, but some privacy and shade are provided by towering lodgepole pines. Just under 200 serviced (powered) sites are grouped together at the end of the road. In addition to hookups, this section has showers and flush toilets; $38. Across the river are 216 unserviced sites, each with a fire ring and picnic table. Other amenities include kitchen shelters and a modern bathroom complex complete with hot showers. These cost $34 per night. A dump station is near the entrance to the campground ($8 per use). An interpretive program runs throughout summer, nightly at 9 P.M. (except Tuesday) in the outdoor theater. Sites can be booked in advance by contacting the **Parks Canada Campground Reservation Service** (877/737-3783, www.pccamping.ca). The many sites available on a first-come, first-served basis fill fast in July and August, so plan on arriving early in the afternoon to ensure a spot. The serviced section of this campground is open year-round, the unserviced section mid-May–September.

FOOD

Other guidebooks encourage readers to "eat at your hotel." Not only is this unhelpful, it's misleading—the village of Lake Louise may exist only to serve travelers, but there are good dining options serving all budgets.

Breakfast

Please don't eat breakfast at the gas station restaurant simply because it is the first place you spot coming off the highway. If you don't feel like a cooked breakfast, start your day off at **❰ Laggan's Mountain Bakery** (Samson Mall, 403/552-2017, 6 A.M.–8 P.M. daily), *the* place to hang out with a coffee and a freshly baked breakfast croissant, pastry, cake, or muffin. The chocolate brownie is delicious (order two slices to save having to line up twice). If the tables are full, order takeout and enjoy your feast on the riverbank behind the mall.

Across the TransCanada Highway, the **Lodge of the Ten Peaks,** at the base of Lake Louise winter resort (403/522-3555), is open in 7:30–10:30 A.M. daily in summer for a large and varied breakfast buffet that costs a super-reasonable adult $13, child $9. An even better

Drop by Laggan's Mountain Bakery for a coffee.

© ANDREW HEMPSTEAD

deal is to purchase a breakfast/gondola ride combo for $26 (the gondola ride alone is $23). The buffet lunch (11:30 A.M.–2:30 P.M.) is $17, or $33 with the gondola ride.

If you made the effort to rise early and experienced the early-morning tranquility of Moraine Lake, the perfect place to sit back and watch the tour-bus crowds pour in is from the dining room of **❰ Moraine Lake Lodge** (403/522-3733, from 7:30 A.M. daily June–Sept.). Staying overnight at the lodge may be an extravagant splurge, but breakfast isn't. A simple, well-presented continental buffet is just $15, while the hot version is a reasonable $18.

European

In 1987, the **❰ Post Hotel** (200 Pipestone Dr., 403/522-3989) was expanded to include a luxurious new wing. The original log building was renovated as a rustic, timbered dining room (6:30–10 P.M. daily) linked to the rest of the hotel by an intimate lounge. Although the dining room isn't cheap, it's a favorite of locals and visitors alike. The chef specializes

ANDREW HEMPSTEAD

Bill Peyto's Cafe

in European cuisine, preparing several Swiss dishes (such as veal zurichois) to make owner George Schwarz feel less homesick. But he's also renowned for his presentation of Alberta beef, Pacific salmon, and Peking duck. Main meals start at $31. The 32,000-bottle cellar is one of the finest in Canada. Reservations are essential for dinner.

Canadian Contemporary

One hundred years ago, visitors departing trains at Laggan Station were eager to get to the Chateau Lake Louise as quickly as possible to begin their adventure. Today, guests from the château, other hotels, and even people from as far away as Banff are returning to dine in the ◖ **Lake Louise Railway Station Restaurant** (200 Sentinel Rd., 403/522-2600, $16–34), which combines a dining room in the actual station (11:30 A.M.–9 P.M. daily) with two restored dining cars (6–9 P.M. Fri.–Sat.). Although the menu is not extensive, it puts an emphasis on creating imaginative dishes with a combination of Canadian produce and

Asian ingredients. Lighter lunches include a Caesar salad topped with roasted garlic dressing ($8.50)—perfect for those planning an afternoon hike. In the evening, expect entrées like a memorable pan-seared salmon smothered in basil pesto.

Samson Mall and Vicinity

In the center of the action, Samson Mall is a hive of activity each afternoon as campers descend on a single grocery store to stock up on supplies for the evening meal. Prices are high, and by the end of the day stocks are low. The mall is also home to **Laggan's,** an ice cream parlor, a small café, and a liquor store. Upstairs in the mall is the **Lake Louise Village Grill & Bar** (403/522-3879). The tiled entrance looks like a public washroom, and the food's ordinary. For a casual meal, much better is **Bill Peyto's Cafe** in the Lake Louise Alpine Centre (Village Rd., 403/522-2200, 7 A.M.–9 P.M. daily, $10–15). The food is consistent and well priced. A huge portion of nachos is $8, pasta is $10–14, and stir-fries range $12–15.

Fairmont Chateau Lake Louise

Within this famous lakeside hotel is a choice of eateries and an ice-cream shop. For all château dining reservations, call 403/522-1817.

The **Poppy Brasserie** has obscured lake views and is the most casual place for a meal. Breakfasts (7–11:30 A.M. daily), offered buffet-style ($28 per person), are a little expensive for light eaters. Lunch and dinner (11:30 A.M.–8:30 P.M. daily, $18.50–32) are à la carte. The **Walliser Stube** (6–9 P.M. daily) is an elegant two-story wine bar decorated with rich wood paneling and solid oak furniture. It offers a simple menu of German dishes from $21 as well as cheese fondue. The **Lakeview Lounge** (noon–4 P.M. daily) has floor-to-ceiling windows with magnificent lake views. Choose this dining area for afternoon tea (noon–4 P.M. daily, reservations required, $31 per person, or $39 with a glass of champagne).

The **Fairview Dining Room** (6–9 P.M. daily, $27–37) has a lot more than just a fair view. As the château's signature dining room, it enjoys the best views and offers the most elegant setting.

INFORMATION AND SERVICES
Information

Lake Louise Visitor Centre (403/522-3833, 8 A.M.–8 P.M. daily mid-June–Aug., 8 A.M.–6 P.M. daily mid-May–mid-June and Sept., 9 A.M.–4 P.M. daily the rest of the year) is beside Samson Mall on Village Road. This excellent Parks Canada facility has interpretive displays, slide and video displays, and staff on hand to answer questions, recommend hikes suited to your ability, and issue camping passes to those heading out into the backcountry. Look for the stuffed (literally) female grizzly and read her fascinating, but sad, story.

Services

A small postal outlet in Samson Mall also serves as a bus depot and car rental agency. Although Lake Louise has no banks, there's a currency exchange in the Fairmont Chateau Lake Louise and a cash machine in the grocery store. The mall also holds a busy laundry

© ANDREW HEMPSTEAD

Wilson Mountain Sports has bike rentals and more.

(8 A.M.–8 P.M. daily in summer, shorter hours the rest of the year). Camping supplies and bike rentals are available from **Wilson Mountain Sports** (403/522-3636, 9 A.M.–9 P.M. daily).

The closest **hospital** is in Banff (403/762-2222). For the local **RCMP,** call 403/522-3811.

GETTING THERE

Calgary International Airport is the closest airport to Lake Louise. **Brewster** (403/762-6767 or 800/661-1152, www.brewster.ca) and **Banff Airporter** (403/762-3330 or 888/449-2901, www.banffairporter.com) offer at least a couple of shuttles per day that continue beyond Banff to Lake Louise from the airport. All charge around the same—$70 each way, with a slight round-trip discount.

Greyhound (403/522-3870) leaves the Calgary bus depot (877 Greyhound Way SW) five times daily for Lake Louise. The fare is less than that charged by Brewster, and the Banff-Lake Louise portion only is around $15. From Vancouver, it's a 13-hour ride to Lake Louise aboard the Greyhound bus.

GETTING AROUND

Samson Mall is the commercial heart of Lake Louise village. If the parking lot out front is full, consider leaving your vehicle across the road behind the Esso gas station, where one area is set aside for large RVs. The campground, alpine center, and hotels are all within easy walking distance of Samson Mall. Fairmont Chateau Lake Louise is a 2.7-kilometer (1.7-mile) walk from the valley floor. The only car-rental agency in the village is **National** (403/522-3870). The agency doesn't have many vehicles; you'd be better off picking one up at Calgary International Airport. **Lake Louise Taxi & Tours** (Samson Mall, 403/522-2020) charges $3 for flag drop, then $1.85 per kilometer. From the mall to Fairmont Chateau Lake Louise runs around $15, to Moraine Lake $35, and to Banff $165. **Wilson Mountain Sports** (Samson Mall, 403/522-3636) has mountain bikes for rent from $15 per hour or $45 per day (includes a helmet, bike lock, and water bottle). They also rent camping, climbing, and fishing gear.

Icefields Parkway (Banff)

The 230-kilometer (143-mile) Icefields Parkway, between Lake Louise and Jasper, is one of the most scenic, exciting, and inspiring mountain roads ever built. From Lake Louise it parallels the Continental Divide, following in the shadow of the highest, most rugged mountains in the Canadian Rockies. The first 122 kilometers (76 miles) to Sunwapta Pass (the boundary between Banff and Jasper National Parks) can be driven in two hours, and the entire parkway in four hours. But it's likely you'll want to spend at least a day, probably more, stopping at each of the 13 viewpoints, hiking the trails, watching the abundant wildlife, and just generally enjoying one of the world's most magnificent landscapes. Along the section within Banff National Park are two lodges, three hostels, three campgrounds, and one gas station.

Although the road is steep and winding in places, it has a wide shoulder, making it ideal for an extended bike trip. Allow seven days to pedal north from Banff to Jasper, staying at hostels or camping along the route. This is the preferable direction to travel by bike because the elevation at the town of Jasper is more than 500 meters (1,640 feet) lower than either Banff or Lake Louise.

The parkway remains open year-round, although winter brings with it some special considerations. The road is often closed for short periods for avalanche control—check road conditions in Banff or Lake Louise before setting out. And be sure to fill up with gas; no services are available between November and April.

SIGHTS AND DRIVES
Lake Louise to Crowfoot Glacier

The Icefields Parkway forks right from the TransCanada Highway just north of Lake Louise. The impressive scenery begins immediately. Just three kilometers (1.9 miles) from the junction is **Herbert Lake,** formed during the last ice age when retreating glaciers deposited a pile of rubble—known as a *moraine*—across a shallow valley and water filled in behind it. The lake is a perfect place for early-morning or early-evening photography, when the Waputik Range and distinctively shaped **Mount Temple** are reflected in its waters.

Traveling north, you'll notice numerous depressions in the steep, shaded slopes of the Waputik Range across the Bow Valley. The cooler climate on these north-facing slopes makes them prone to glaciation. Cirques were cut by small local glaciers. On the opposite side of the road, **Mount Hector** (3,394 meters/11,130 feet), easily recognized by its layered peak, soon comes into view.

Hector Lake Viewpoint is 16 kilometers (10 miles) from the junction. Although the view is partially obscured by trees, the emerald green waters nestled below a massive wall of limestone form a breathtaking scene. **Bow Peak,** seen looking northward along the highway, is only 2,868 meters (9,410 feet) high but is completely detached from the Waputik Range, making it a popular destination for climbers. As you leave this viewpoint, look across the northeast end of Hector Lake for glimpses of **Mount Balfour** (3,246 meters/10,650 feet) on the distant skyline.

Crowfoot Glacier

The aptly named Crowfoot Glacier can best be appreciated from a viewpoint 17 kilometers (10.6 miles) north of Hector Lake. The glacier sits on a wide ledge near the top of Crowfoot Mountain, from where its glacial claws cling to the mountain's steep slopes. The retreat of this glacier has been dramatic. Only 50 years ago, two of the claws extended to the base of the lower cliff. Today, they are a shadow of their former selves, barely reaching over the cliff edge.

Bow Lake

◖ Bow Lake

The sparkling, translucent waters of Bow Lake are among the most beautiful that can be seen from the Icefields Parkway. The lake was created when moraines deposited by retreating glaciers dammed subsequent meltwater. On still days, the water reflects the snowy peaks, their sheer cliffs, and the scree slopes that run into the lake. You don't need photography experience to take good pictures here! At the southeast end of the lake, a day-use area offers waterfront picnic tables and a trail to a swampy area at the lake's outlet. At the upper end of the lake, you'll find the historic Num-ti-jah Lodge and the trailhead for a walk to Bow Glacier Falls.

The road leaves Bow Lake and climbs to **Bow Summit.** As you look back toward the lake, its true color becomes apparent, and the Crowfoot Glacier reveals its unique shape. At an elevation of 2,069 meters (6,790 feet), this pass is one of the highest points crossed by a public road in Canada. It is also the beginning of the Bow River, the one you camped beside at Lake Louise, photographed flowing through the town of Banff, and fished along downstream of Canmore.

◖ Peyto Lake

From the parking lot at Bow Summit, a short paved trail leads to one of the most breathtaking views you could ever imagine. Far below the viewpoint is Peyto Lake, an impossibly intense green lake whose hues change according to season. Before heavy melting of nearby glaciers begins (in June or early July), the lake is dark blue. As summer progresses, meltwater flows across a delta and into the lake. This water is laden with finely ground particles of rock debris known as rock flour, which remains suspended in the water. It is not the mineral content of the rock flour that is responsible for the lake's unique color, but rather the particles reflecting the blue-green sector of the light spectrum. As the amount of suspended rock flour changes, so does the color of the lake.

The lake is one of many park landmarks named for early outfitter Bill Peyto. In 1898, Peyto was part of an expedition camped at Bow Lake. Seeking solitude (as he was wont to do), he slipped off during the night to sleep near this lake. Other members of the party coined the name Peyto's Lake, and it stuck.

© ANDREW HEMPSTEAD

Peyto Lake

A farther three kilometers (1.9 miles) along the parkway is a viewpoint from which **Peyto Glacier** is visible at the far end of Peyto Lake Valley. This glacier is part of the extensive **Wapta Icefield,** which straddles the Continental Divide and extends into the northern reaches of Yoho National Park in British Columbia.

Beside the Continental Divide

From Bow Summit, the parkway descends to a viewpoint directly across the Mistaya River from **Mount Patterson** (3,197 meters/10,490 feet). Snowbird Glacier clings precariously to the mountain's steep northeast face, and the mountain's lower, wooded slopes are heavily scarred where rock and ice slides have swept down the mountainside.

As the parkway continues to descend and crosses Silverhorn Creek, the jagged limestone peaks of the Continental Divide can be seen to the west. **Mistaya Lake** is a three-kilometer-long (1.9-mile-long) body of water that sits at the bottom of the valley between the road and the divide, but it can't be seen from the parkway. The best place to view it is from the Howse Peak

Viewpoint at Upper Waterfowl Lake. From here the high ridge that forms the Continental Divide is easily distinguishable. Seven peaks can be seen from here, including **Howse Peak** (3,290 meters/10,790 feet). At no point along this ridge does the elevation drop below 2,750 meters (9,000 feet). From Howse Peak, the Continental Divide makes a 90-degree turn to the west. One dominant peak that can be seen from Bow Pass to north of Saskatchewan River Crossing is **Mount Chephren** (3,268 meters/10,720 feet). Its distinctive shape and position away from the main ridge of the Continental Divide make it easy to distinguish. (Look for it directly north of Howse Peak.)

To Saskatchewan River Crossing

Numerous trails lead around the swampy shores of **Upper** and **Lower Waterfowl Lakes,** providing one of the park's best opportunities to view moose, who feed on the abundant aquatic vegetation that grows in Upper Waterfowl Lake. Rock and other debris that have been carried down nearby valley systems have built up, forming a wide alluvial fan, nearly blocking the Mistaya River and creating Upper Waterfowl Lake.

Continuing north is **Mount Murchison** (3,337 meters/10,950 feet), on the east side of the parkway. Although not one of the park's highest mountains, this gray and yellow massif of Cambrian rock comprises 10 individual peaks, covering an area of 3,000 hectares (7,400 acres).

From a parking lot 14 kilometers (8.9 miles) northeast of Waterfowl Lake Campground, a short trail descends into the montane forest to **Mistaya Canyon.** Here the effects of erosion can be appreciated as the Mistaya River leaves the floor of Mistaya Valley, plunging through a narrow-walled canyon into the North Saskatchewan Valley. The area is scarred with potholes where boulders have been whirled around by the action of fast-flowing water, carving deep depressions into the softer limestone bedrock below.

The **North Saskatchewan River** posed a major problem for early travelers and later for the builders of the Icefields Parkway. This swiftly running river eventually drains into Hudson Bay. In 1989 it was named a Canadian Heritage River. One kilometer (0.6 mile) past the bridge you'll come to a panoramic viewpoint of the entire valley. From here the Howse and Mistaya Rivers can be seen converging with the North Saskatchewan at a silt-laden delta. This is also a junction with Highway 11 (also known as David Thompson Highway), which follows the North Saskatchewan River to Rocky Mountain House and Red Deer. From this viewpoint numerous peaks can be seen to the west. Two sharp peaks are distinctive: **Mount Outram** (3,254 meters/10,680 feet) is the closer; the farther is **Mount Forbes** (3,630 meters/11,975 feet), the highest peak in Banff National Park (and the sixth highest in the Canadian Rockies).

To Sunwapta Pass

On the north side of the North Saskatchewan River is the towering hulk of **Mount Wilson** (3,261 meters/10,700 feet), named for Banff outfitter Tom Wilson. The Icefields Parkway passes this massif on its western flanks. A pullout just past Rampart Creek Campground offers good views of Mount Amery to the west and Mounts Sarbach, Chephren, and Murchison to the south. Beyond here is the **Weeping Wall,** a long cliff of gray limestone where a series of waterfalls tumbles more than 100 meters (330 feet) down the steep slopes of Cirrus Mountain. In winter this wall of water freezes, becoming a mecca for ice climbers.

After ascending quickly, the road drops again before beginning a long climb to Sunwapta Pass. Halfway up the 360-vertical-meter (1,180-vertical-foot) climb is a viewpoint well worth a stop (cyclists will definitely appreciate a rest). From here views extend down the valley to the slopes of Mount Saskatchewan and, on the other side of the parkway, Cirrus Mountain. Another viewpoint, farther up the road, has the added attraction of a view of Panther Falls across the valley. A cairn at **Sunwapta Pass** (2,023 meters/6,640 feet) marks the boundary between Banff and Jasper National Parks. It also marks the divide between the North Saskatchewan and Sunwapta Rivers, whose waters drain into the Atlantic and Arctic Oceans, respectively.

HIKING
Helen Lake

- Length: 6 kilometers/3.7 miles (2.5 hours) one-way
- Elevation gain: 455 meters/1,500 feet
- Rating: moderate
- Trailhead: across the Icefields Parkway from Crowfoot Glacier Lookout, 33 kilometers (20 miles) northwest from the junction with the TransCanada Highway

The trail to Helen Lake is one of the easiest ways to access a true alpine environment from the southern end of the Icefields Parkway. The trail climbs steadily through a forest of Engelmann spruce and subalpine fir for the first 2.5 kilometers (1.6 miles) to an avalanche slope, reaching the tree line and the first good viewpoint after three kilometers (1.9 miles). The view across the valley is spectacular, with Crowfoot Glacier visible to the southwest. As the trail reaches a ridge, it turns and descends into the glacial cirque where Helen Lake lies. Listen and look for hoary marmots around the scree slopes along the lakeshore.

For those with the time and energy, it's possible to continue an additional three kilometers (1.9 miles) to Dolomite Pass; the trail switchbacks steeply up a further 100 vertical meters (330 vertical feet) in less than one kilometer (0.6 mile), then descends steeply for a further one kilometer (0.6 mile) to Katherine Lake and beyond to the pass.

Bow Glacier Falls

- Length: 3.4 kilometers/2.1 miles (1 hour) one-way
- Elevation gain: 130 meters/430 feet
- Rating: easy
- Trailhead: Num-ti-jah Lodge, Bow Lake, 36 kilometers (22.3 miles) northwest from the TransCanada Highway

This hike skirts one of the most beautiful lakes in the Canadian Rockies before ending at a narrow but spectacular waterfall. From the parking lot in front of Num-ti-jah Lodge, follow the shore through Willow Flats to a gravel outwash area at the end of the lake. Across the lake are reflected views of Crowfoot Mountain and, farther west, a glimpse of Bow Glacier among the jagged peaks of the Waputik Range. The trail then begins a short but steep climb up the rim of a canyon before leveling out at the edge of a vast moraine of gravel, scree, and boulders. This is the end of the trail, although it's possible to reach the base of Bow Glacier Falls by picking your way through the 800 meters (0.5 mile) of rough ground that remains.

Peyto Lake

- Length: 1.4 kilometers/0.9 mile (30 minutes) one-way
- Elevation loss: 100 meters/330 feet
- Rating: easy
- Trailhead: unmarked pullout, Icefields Parkway, 2.4 kilometers (1.5 miles) north of Bow Summit

Without a doubt, the best place to view Peyto Lake is from a popular viewpoint accessible via a short trail from Bow Summit, 41 kilometers (25.5 miles) along the Icefields Parkway from the TransCanada Highway. The easiest way to access the actual shoreline, though, is along this short trail farther along the highway. A pebbled beach, strewn with driftwood, is the perfect setting for picnicking, painting, or just admiring the lake's quieter side. Back at the lake lookout, a rough trail drops nearly 300 meters (980 feet) in 2.4 kilometers (1.5 miles) to the lake.

Chephren Lake

- Length: 4 kilometers/2.5 miles (60–90 minutes) one-way
- Elevation gain: 100 meters/330 feet
- Rating: easy
- Trailhead: Waterfowl Lake Campground, Icefields Parkway, 57 kilometers (35 miles) northwest from the TransCanada Highway

This pale-green body of water (pronounced Kef-ren) is hidden from the Icefields Parkway but easily reached. The official trailhead is a

Walk down to the shoreline for a close-up view of the famous Peyto Lake.

bridge across the Mistaya River at the back of Waterfowl Lakes Campground (behind site 86). If you're not registered at the campground, park at the end of the unpaved road running along the front of the campground and walk 300 meters (0.2 mile) down the well-worn path to the river crossing. From across the river, the trail dives headlong into a subalpine forest, reaching a crudely signposted junction after 1.6 kilometers (one mile). Take the right fork. This leads 2.4 kilometers (1.5 miles) to Chephren Lake, descending steeply at the end (this stretch of trail is often muddy). The lake is nestled under the buttresses of Mount Chephren. To the left—farther up the lake—is Howse Peak.

The trail to smaller **Cirque Lake** (4.5 km/2.8 miles from the trailhead) branches left 1.6 kilometers (one mile) along this trail. It is less heavily used, but this lake is popular with anglers for its healthy population of rainbow trout.

Glacier Lake

- Length: 9 kilometers/5.6 miles (2.5–3 hours) one-way
- Elevation gain: 220 meters/770 feet
- Rating: moderate
- Trailhead: an old gravel pit on the west side of the highway, 1 kilometer (0.6 mile) west of Saskatchewan River Crossing

This three-kilometer-long (1.9-mile-long) lake is one of the park's largest lakes not accessible by road. Although not as scenic as the more accessible lakes along the parkway, it's a pleasant destination for a full-day or overnight trip. For the first one kilometer (0.6 mile), the trail passes through an open forest of lodgepole pine to a fancy footbridge across the rushing North Saskatchewan River. From there it climbs gradually to a viewpoint overlooking Howse River and the valley beyond, then turns away from the river for a long slog through dense forest to Glacier Lake. A primitive campground lies just over 300 meters (0.2 mile) from where the trail emerges at the lake.

Saskatchewan Glacier

- Length: 7.3 kilometers/4.5 miles (2 hours) one-way
- Elevation gain: 150 meters/490 feet
- Rating: moderate
- Trailhead: small parking lot, 35 kilometers (22 miles) northwest of the Saskatchewan River Crossing (just before the highway begins its "Big Bend" up to Sunwapta Pass)

The Saskatchewan Glacier, a tongue of ice from the great Columbia Icefield, is visible from various points along the Icefields Parkway. This hike will take you right to the toe of the glacier. After crossing an old concrete bridge, the trail disappears into the forest to the right, joining an overgrown road and continuing up the valley along the south bank of the river. When the toe of the glacier first comes into sight it looks deceptively close, but it's still a long hike away over rough terrain.

Nigel Pass

- Length: 7.4 kilometers/4.6 miles (2.5 hours) one-way
- Elevation gain: 365 meters/1,200 feet
- Rating: moderate
- Trailhead: Icefields Parkway, 2.5 kilometers (1.6 miles) north of the switchback on the "Big Bend"

Park on the east side of the highway and follow the gravel road to a locked gate. Turn right here and cross Nigel Creek on the bridge. The trail is obvious, following open avalanche paths up the east side of the valley. In a stand of Engelmann spruce and subalpine fir two kilometers (1.2 miles) from the trailhead is an old campsite used first by native hunting parties, then by mountaineers exploring the area around the Columbia Icefield. Look for carvings on trees recording these early visitors. From here the trail continues to climb steadily, only increasing in gradient for the last one kilometer (0.6 mile) to the pass. The pass (2,195 meters/7,200 feet) marks the boundary between Banff and Jasper National Parks. For the best view, scramble over the rocks to the left. To the north, the view extends down the Brazeau River Valley, surrounded by a mass of peaks. To the west (left) is Nigel Peak (3,211 meters/10,535 feet), and to the southwest are views of Parker's Ridge and the glaciated peaks of Mount Athabasca.

Parker's Ridge

* Length: 2.4 kilometers/1.5 miles (1 hour) one-way

* Elevation gain: 210 meters/690 feet

* Rating: easy/moderate

* Trailhead: Icefields Parkway, 4 kilometers (2.5 miles) south of Sunwapta Pass

From the trailhead on the west side of the highway, this wide path gains elevation quickly through open meadows and scattered stands of subalpine fir. This fragile environment is easily destroyed, so it's important that you stay on the trail. During the short alpine summer, these meadows are carpeted with red heather, white mountain avens, and blue alpine forget-me-nots. From the summit of the ridge, you look down on the two-kilometer-wide (1.2-mile-wide) Saskatchewan Glacier spreading out below. Beyond is Castleguard Mountain, renowned for its extensive cave system.

ACCOMMODATIONS AND CAMPING
Under $50

North of Lake Louise, four hostels are spread along the Icefields Parkway, two in Banff and two in Jasper National Park. Facilities at all four are limited, and beds should be reserved as far in advance as possible. For reservations, call 778/328-2220 or 866/762-4122, or book online (www.hihostels.ca). The first, 24 kilometers (15 miles) from Lake Louise, is **HI-Mosquito Creek**, which is near good hiking and offers accommodations for 32 in four- and six-bed cabins. Facilities include a kitchen, wood-heated sauna, and a large common room with fireplace. Although the hostel has

no showers, guests are permitted to use those at the nearby Lake Louise Alpine Centre. Rates are $23 per night for members of Hostelling International; nonmembers pay $27. Check-in is 5–10 P.M., and it's open June–March.

HI-Rampart Creek, a further 64 kilometers (40 miles) along the parkway, is nestled below the snowcapped peak of Mount Wilson, with views across the North Saskatchewan River to even higher peaks along the Continental Divide. Like Mosquito Creek, it's near good hiking and has a kitchen and sauna. Its four cabins have a total of 24 bunk beds. Members pay $23 per night, nonmembers $27. It's open nightly May–March. Check-in is 5–10 P.M.

$50-150

The Crossing Resort (403/761-7000, www.thecrossingresort.com, April–Nov., $159–209 s or d) is a large complex 87 kilometers (54 miles) north of Lake Louise and 45 kilometers (28 miles) south of Columbia Icefield. It's also one kilometer (0.6 mile) north of Saskatchewan River Crossing, where Highway 11 spurs east along Abraham Lake to Rocky Mountain House and Red Deer. The rooms offer a good combination of size and value but lack the historic charm of those at Num-ti-jah to the south and the views enjoyed by those at the Columbia Icefield Centre to the north. Each of 66 units has a phone and television. All rates are heavily discounted outside of June–September. In addition to overnight rooms, The Crossing has the only gas between Lake Louise and Jasper, a self-serve cafeteria, a restaurant, a pub with a cook-your-own-steak grill, and a supersized gift shop.

Over $150

Pioneer guide and outfitter Jimmy Simpson built **ℂ Simpson's Num-ti-jah Lodge** (403/522-2167, www.num-ti-jah.com, from $320 s or d), on the north shore of Bow Lake, 40 kilometers (25 miles) north of Lake Louise, as a base for his outfitting operation in 1920. In those days, the route north from Lake Louise was nothing more than a horse trail. The desire to build a large structure when

© ANDREW HEMPSTEAD

Simpson's Num-ti-jah Lodge

only short timbers were available led to the unusual octagonal shape of the main lodge. Simpson remained at Bow Lake, a living legend, until his death in 1972 at the age of 95. With a rustic mountain ambience that has changed little since Simpson's passing, Num-ti-jah will provide a memorable overnight stay. Just don't expect the conveniences of a regular motel. Under the distinctively red, steep-pitched roof of the main lodge are 25 rooms, some that share bathrooms, and there's not a TV or phone in sight. Downstairs, guests soak up the warmth of a roaring log fire while mingling in a comfortable library filled with historic mountain literature. A dining room lined with historic memorabilia is open daily for breakfast and dinner.

Campgrounds

Beyond Lake Louise, the first camping along the Icefields Parkway is at **Mosquito Creek Campground** (year-round, $21), 24 kilometers (15 miles) from the TransCanada Highway. Don't be perturbed by the name, though; the bugs here are no worse than anywhere else. The 32 sites are nestled in the forest, with a tumbling creek separating the campground from a hostel. Each site has a picnic table and fire ring, while other amenities include pump water, pit toilets, and a kitchen shelter with an old-fashioned woodstove. If you're camping at Mosquito Creek and want a break from the usual camp fare, consider traveling 17 kilometers (10.6 miles) up the highway to the convivial dining room at Num-ti-jah Lodge (403/522-2167) to feast on Canadian-inspired cuisine in a historic dining room.

Waterfowl Lake Campground (late June–mid-Sept., $27) is 33 kilometers (20 miles) north along the Icefields Parkway from Mosquito Creek. It features 116 sites between Upper and Lower Waterfowl Lakes, with a few sites in view of the lower lake. Facilities include pump water, flush toilets, and kitchen shelters with wood-burning stoves. Rise early to watch the first rays of sun hit Mount Chephren from the shoreline of the lower lake, then plan on hiking the four-kilometer (2.5-mile) trail to Chephren Lake—you'll be first on the trail and back in time for a late breakfast.

Continuing toward Jasper, the Icefields Parkway passes The Crossing, a good place to gas up and buy last-minute groceries before reaching **Rampart Creek Campground** (late June–early Sept., $21 per site), 31 kilometers (19 miles) beyond Waterfowl Lake and 88 kilometers (55 miles) from Lake Louise. With just 50 sites, this campground fills early. Facilities include kitchen shelters, pit toilets, and pump water.

MOON BANFF NATIONAL PARK

Avalon Travel
a member of the Perseus Books Group
1700 Fourth Street
Berkeley, CA 94710, USA
www.moon.com

Editor: Erin Raber
Series Manager: Kathryn Ettinger
Copy Editor: Justine Rathbun
Graphics and Production Coordinator:
   Elizabeth Jang
Cover Designer: Kathryn Osgood
Map Editor: Albert Angulo
Cartographer: Kat Bennett

ISBN-13: 978-1-59880-556-7

Front cover photo: Moraine Lake, Banff National Park,
© Ketian Chen | Dreamstime.com
Title page: © Andrew Hempstead

Printed in the United States

ABOUT THE AUTHOR

Andrew Hempstead

As a travel writer and photographer, Andrew Hempstead has spent many years exploring, photographing, and writing about Canada. He looks forward to spending every second summer at home in the Canadian Rockies, traveling mountain highways and hiking trails, exploring new places and updating old favorites. He spends as much time as possible on the road, traveling incognito, experiencing the many and varied delights of the region just as his readers do.

Andrew has been writing since the late 1980s, when he left an established career in advertising and took off for Alaska, linking up with veteran travel writer Deke Castleman to research and update the fourth edition of the Moon Handbook to Alaska and the Yukon. Since then he has produced several guides to Canada, including guidebooks to British Columbia, Vancouver and Victoria, Alberta, Western Canada, Atlantic Canada, and Nova Scotia. He is also the author of Moon guidebooks to Australia and New Zealand, and a contributor to *Moon San Juan Islands, Road Trip USA, Northwest Best Places,* and *Eyewitness Guide to the USA,* as well as the update of *The Illustrated Guide to New Zealand.* His writing and photographs have appeared in a wide variety of other media, including *National Geographic Traveler, Travesias, Where, Interval World,* Microsoft's *Automap,* and on the Alaska Airlines and Expedia websites.

The website www.westerncanadatravel.com showcases Andrew's work, while also providing invaluable planning tips for travelers heading to Canada.